IT'S YOU I LOVE

Testimonies of Miraculous Healings
and Deliverances From God

BILLY DAVISON

WESTBOW
PRESS®
A DIVISION OF THOMAS NELSON
& ZONDERVAN

WestBow Press books may be ordered through booksellers or by contacting:

WestBow Press
A Division of Thomas Nelson & Zondervan
1663 Liberty Drive
Bloomington, IN 47403
www.westbowpress.com
844-714-3454

Scripture taken from the King James Version of the Bible.

Scripture taken from the New King James Version® Copyright © 1982 by Thomas Nelson. Used by permission. All rights reserved.

Scripture quotations taken from The Holy Bible, New International Version® NIV® Copyright © 1973 1978 1984 2011 by Biblica, Inc. TM. Used by permission. All rights reserved worldwide.

ISBN: 978-1-6642-2136-9 (sc)
ISBN: 978-1-6642-2137-6 (e)

Library of Congress Control Number: 2021901703

Print information available on the last page.

WestBow Press rev. date: 01/25/2021

Contents

Foreword

written by Pastor Michael Floyd

When I first met Billy Davison I admit I looked at him after the flesh. I literally thought of him as John the Baptist with his hairy beard. I looked to see if there was a piece of locust and honey smeared in his beard! But, like I say I was looking at him after the flesh, and not after the spirit. I love his humor and how quick-witted he is. To tell the truth, he made me laugh and still does. But then God reminded me of I Samuel 16:7 of what the Lord said to Samuel about David's brother Eliab, "For the Lord seeth not as a man seeth, for man looketh on the outward appearance but the Lord looketh on the heart."

So I began to look at Billy's heart, and God showed me he was like a precious diamond in the rough. Outside he may have appeared afraid, disappointed, and frustrated, but on the inside he is like David, God's anointed and appointed. I could see the call of God on his life, and that God really wanted to use him in His Kingdom and for His Glory. I began to see that God had given him some amazing gifts in the spirit, but no one saw that potential he had in Christ. The Lord told me you must help this man, because he is a chosen vessel unto me. I have begun a good work in him, and I was to help him to reach his potential in Christ.

The farther I looked inside Billy, I began to see what God saw in him. It thrilled me to see that God had sent him to me to help bring out that beautiful gem or diamond that is in him. And like all of us, God uses us not because we are perfect, but because we have surrendered to Him. And like that clay on the wheel, He is perfecting us.

I have been with Billy ministering to people and have witnessed first hand the love of God flowing out of him to others. I have watched him give words of knowledge and words of wisdom, and prophesy over people and literally read their mail. I have personally seen how God has used him with the gifts of healing, and at times working of miracles.

Billy came to me several months ago and told me the Lord told him to write a book about the Love of God. I had already noticed that he had a God-given gift to write. I know that he will make an impact on this world as long as he stays true to the Lord and His Word, and allows God to use him in every way possible. I heard the Lord say to me, watch what I will do with him and through him.

I consider Billy one of my trusted friends, and I am like a spiritual father to a spiritual son. I am so humbled and blessed to see what God is going to do with this diamond in the rough. I am blessed and thankful to call him my brother in the Lord.

In Christ,
Bro Mike Floyd

Dedication

I want to first thank God, for helping me find my way in the dark. "Give thanks in all circumstances; for this is God's will for you in Christ Jesus."1 Thessalonians 5:18. NKJV

Second, I want to thank my wife, Terrie Kay, she deserves a medal! I never promised, our life would always be a paradise; but I did promise that through thick and thin, I would love you to the best of my abilities. I apologize that I could not give you the castle you deserved, but I'm blessed that you never left my side, when you had every right to. I thank God for bringing you to me and keeping you there when times were tough and life was hard. For 26 years I've loved you, and for the next 25 years I'll do my best to prove to you that I do. Thank you for the smiles and the laughter and our three beautiful children. I am truly blessed. Terrie Kay I love you!

Thank you to my three beautiful children, Tanisha Jo, Taylor Ann, and Dusty Wyatt. And to many of my family and friends. One for helping me with the stories and testimonies and two for being patient with me while I spent long days and hours writing this. God Bless you all; I love you.

This book is dedicated to my Grandchildren. You are my greatest accomplishments!." But Jesus looked at them and said to them, "With men this is impossible, but with God all things are possible." (Matthew 19:26 NKJV) My prayer for you is that you may always walk with the Holy Spirit and in love. Please always choose love. Jesus loves you and so do I. Papa

Because God responded to a sinner's prayer on May 11, 2015. I have had the wonderful opportunity of sharing my testimony of how Great Our Heavenly Father is. People always ask me how can you say you love me, when you don't even know me? And my response is always the same. If people can hate someone, I can love them. I am very blessed to be able to share my story of being a hurt, lost, downtrodden, broken individual who with God I overcame the pitfalls of the world.

Preface

If I'm wrong about believing in the scripture and in Jesus Christ when I die, I'll Lose nothing! However if you're wrong and He really is the King of kings and the Lord of lords; and what He said is true, then when you die you lose everything!

There's a lot of things in the Holy Bible I don't understand, but I believe every word of it. What I do understand is that it enforces my faith in Jesus Christ. Please don't think of Jesus as just a Band-Aid for a temporary cover up of your problems. You are very ignorant and misinformed of the truth of Jesus Christ if you believe that. Ignorant doesn't mean stupid, it means unknowledgeable, uneducated, lacking knowledge or awareness, or unsophisticated. If you don't know the truth, ask.

Jeremiah 33:3 NKJV, says, "Call to Me, and I will answer you, and show you great and mighty things, which you do not know." If you are never taught you will never know and understand this book. The Bible will help remove roadblocks and give you a clear understanding of the greatness of God.

Billy Davison

God Still Heals

It may be cold with the ground covered with snow or raining like the Amazon forest with mud everywhere or perhaps you're somewhere where it's sunny and 80 degrees. Wherever you are I thank the Lord for your safety and giving you another day on this beautiful earthly planet. And to be able to worship and fellowship with him. And be able to share your testimony with others of the great work of the Holy Spirit and what he's done in your life. So how are you doing this moment?

Well to tell you the truth I'm tired, my back hurts, the kids are leaving the house a mess before heading off to school and on and on and on.

Remember Proverbs 17:22 NKJV tells us, "A merry heart does good, like medicine, But a broken spirit dries the bones." Well, however your day started we'll have some kind of complaint, but the majority of the time we never have a thank you Lord. I know we all fall short at times. As soon as we open our eyes to the sound of the birds chirping or the neighbors dog barking or car alarms honking or the annoying alarm clock going off. We do not stop and thank God for giving us another day and thank him for the beauty that surrounds us. The scripture says in James 4:14 NKJV "Whereas you do not know what will happen tomorrow. For what is your life? It is even a vapor that appears for a little time and then vanishes away." Very powerful verse.

The purpose of this book was inspired by the Holy Spirit. It was written to give you encouragement that God is still healing this very hour and through these testimonies you'll see He's Not a respecter of persons. If He'll do it for one He'll do it for you as is stated in Acts 10:34 (NKJV). I am Completely open, honest and forthright about my sinful past. I'm not proud of the things I did. Neither am I boastful of them. I can't go back and change anything or alter anything of the past. All I can do is ask for forgiveness from my loving and forgiving Heavenly Father and change my future. These testimonies will give you the inside of how our father, a king, saved this once dirty rotten scoundrel. I have been redeemed by the blood of the Lamb, now I can walk with my head up knowing I've been forgiven by a loving heavenly Father. "For God so loved the world that He gave His only begotten Son, that whoever believes in Him should not perish but have everlasting life.", John 3:16 (NKJV).

So we don't have to live in shame and hide anymore. I now live in the light of a merciful God. People that are not living in a Christian life will never understand the freedom of releasing their burdens of sin and walking in complete forgiveness. All the work and energy it takes to hide their sins, is a full-time job trust me I know. You have to lie to this person about one sin, and lie to a different person about another sin and try to hide all your sins from the world. I hope this book will help you be able to release all those burdens that you are holding inside, and you'll be able to finally release them to God and you'll walk in total forgiveness also. I'm telling you, you'll feel like a brand new person, not a pack mule!

God sees your heart and He's standing right beside you saying, "Let it go and Give it to me". All your problems, all your worries, all your troubles, hand them to the Lord. Don't go another day being bogged down by the troubles of sin. Don't let the devil and his gurus steal any more precious time from you. Don't buy the lies and garbage that he whispers to you. Rebuke him and walk on! God has forgiven you; ask for forgiveness and walk on. You were forgiven by a loving God, accept your forgiveness. Jesus said in John 8:11 (NKJV), "Neither do I condemn you; go and sin no more."

So Let me start with sharing about myself. I was born in January of 1974. I'm telling you this to show you in the eyes of the world I was nothing special, my dad was a truck driver and my mother a housewife. My parents were Pentecostals, neither one working at it very hard. They were a middle class Midwestern typical family. When I came into the world I must have had "butterball" stamped on my chest; I was a pudgy bouncing baby boy. I looked like something they won at the local county fair in the scrambles. Lol

I often joke about coming from a broken home, a tree fell upon it, but in reality there was some truth to it. Because of sinful acts our home was destroyed. But God can use the broken pieces and make a masterpiece. This is my own personal testimony of how God uses avenues and ways to show me He's still in charge and He's always been there to get my attention. God will open up doors and avenues to get us to see his pure Love. Ever since I was old enough to realize or notice that the Holy Spirit had a divine power and plan for my life; like Jonah I ran! This is my story.

From the time I can remember I've been known as a Pentecostal. So praying in tongues, seeing people healed, gifts of prophecy, knowledge and everything described in 1 Corinthians 12 and 13 (NKJV) was always the norm for me. My grandmother was a marvelous intercessor and prayer warrior. She operated in many gifts. As a child, I often wondered if she had a direct phone line to God. People are always going to her for prayer, it was such an awesome sight to see. My grandmother and her two kid sisters had an awesome vast knowledge of God. My biggest regret in life was not embracing all that wonderful knowledge that those three great ladies of God had. Sadly for us they have gone home, and all that wonderful knowledge they had went with them. My advice is if you know an outstanding prayer warrior, you leach on too one of them like a wood tick!! And you learn every single thing you can. Because my friend's there's not many of those left. "Blessed are the pure in heart, For they shall see God." Matthew 5:8 (NKJV)

After I got married going to church seemed like something I never had time for. Before I knew it, life got turned upside down and accidentally I put God on the back burner, without even noticing it. "So that shows my walk with the Lord wasn't where it should have been!" The stresses of being an adult kind of replaces God altogether. Kids come, bills get bigger and we don't even know that we have derailed and moved away from God so far and we are living in the world. As you work so much and wish you can forget all the troubles and cares and move back home. You dream often about the times of making a fort in your room. The only decision you had to make was when you wanted to go to bed. I didn't realize I had fallen so far from the glory of God. It wasn't until my grandmother passed away that my eyes were opened to see how far I had fallen into the world of sin. Isn't life wonderful when everything is going right. But sometimes wonderful can change in a blink of an eye, and it becomes a heartache before we can even understand why.

After her passing, I was mad, hurt and confused about how a loving God could let this happen to one of his great prayer warriors. In April of 1999, that's when I chose to take God out of my life. It was a beautiful Spring day in April when I walked out of the hospital and renounced God! I had never lost anyone so close to me, this was like the biggest death in my young life. I didn't know how to cope with her passing so I let the heartache of her passing start destroying everything I had ever loved. I allowed the devil to come in and set up shop. The rage and unforgiveness, bitterness and anger sent me deeper into the world than I had ever gone before. "It was one of the biggest mistakes and lowest points I had gotten too; and from that point I lived a life full of sin. It was all about me and my pleasures. I had so much hatred in my life that if anybody mentioned my grandmother's name or God I would kick them out of my house. Two people I loved and always found comfort and refuge in I lost at the same time. Instead of getting closer to God I pushed him farther away. I had such a huge hole inside of me and I was inflicting as much pain and hurt to fill it, but it just kept getting bigger. It was because as soon as we push God out of the picture that is an invitation to let the devil and his gurus come in and destroy our life. You have just given him a legal right!

Soon after I renounced God I left my pregnant wife and my baby girl. I had a wonderful doctor who had me hooked on Demerol. From popping pills and drinking booze to picking up women on the corner. I was doing all I could to destroy myself to try to fill up that gaping hole in my soul. My life was so awful I was trying to die like a rockstar. I was so ignorant I was buying into the devil's lies of how useless and worthless I was. I believe to this day the reason why I didn't die was because God had his hand on me. And He knew the great things He had in store for me Jeremiah 29:11 (NKJV) says "For I know the thoughts that I think toward you, says the Lord, thoughts of peace and not of evil, to give you a future and a hope."

Unfortunately, I didn't see what he had in store for me. I was giving my soul away. I had enough. The hurt, the so-called friends, the miserable pain of the absence of a loved one. I was teetering on the fence between good and evil. The fence that separates God and the world. That fence Is owned by the devil, but here's the great news. God is never willing to give up on us! Even though we are away from him, He's going to keep reminding us how much He loves us, because we are all children of an Almighty God! He loves his children so much and like we love our children we have to give them space and room to blow off some steam and make their own mistakes at times. God calls that "free will", but God is always within earshot to say, "Hey, I love you and I forgive you".

I was out on my Harley-Davidson on a cool July evening just four months after the passing of my grandmother and I ran into a cousin who was with a group of friends. This is how awesome Jesus is; He never misses a beat. He's always three steps ahead of us. He allows us to go so far before putting a barricade in our way to get our attention. This cousin was someone I only saw at funerals and wasn't really close to, but he had introduced me to this motorcycle group called the CMA. They were all married couples who loved Jesus Christ and motorcycles. And I had a pretty sweet Harley-Davidson that I loved to show off, so I agreed to go hang out with them for the evening. These people were so friendly and let this raggedy looking stranger in their home with open arms. I sat down on their sofa and we talked about my Harley and other things of no importance. Then the wives came in and joined the conversation and it was like a machine-gun fire of questions. The first question asked, "Do you know God?" I swallowed kind of hard and said next question? Are you married? Again I replied with, next question. Do you have any children? You talk about conviction, I felt it, that day in a little farmhouse. After living in the world for the last four months, those three questions opened my eyes to reveal a few things.

First, God loves this very stupid, stupid man and why; I don't know? Immediately the devil whispers a lie campaign into my ear; God will never forgive you, you renounced Him and then left your family. For once, since April, time felt like it stood still. It felt like hours went by as I was sitting there with this blank stare. With a supernatural war going on inside of my body and several onlookers waiting for an answer to their questions. I did something stupid! What have I done????? What have I done???? What have I done???? I was so upset by the passing of my grandmother, I didn't even consider or realize the physical pain that others were going through also. I was making it worse by the torment and torture of leaving my family. I was so childish and selfish. Oh God what have I done? I didn't think I could say that enough. Oh God what have I done? But it is so awesome how God works in our lives how through one person the door can be opened and meet someone else who can open yet another door. That is why fellowship is needed.

Rev 3:7 (NKJV) "These things says He who is holy, He who is true, "He who has the key of David, He who opens and no one shuts, and shuts and no one opens". As I rode off from their house at night, realizing I never answered those three simple questions they asked. Inside they were being repeated over and over and really working on me. Every time I tried to think of something else they kept returning to my memory.

A cool summer breeze was blowing my hair as I rode down past strip mine lakes back in the town. I couldn't shake those simple questions that were weighing on my heart. Do I know God and am I married? Do you have children? Well it's time to wake up and really be brutally honest with myself. As I pulled into the driveway of my apartment I took my phone off the hook lock the door and looked into the mirror. What am I doing?, Where am I going? Do I know God? After spending Restless hours looking at a pathetic image in the mirror until the early morning sunlight was shining through my window and still I had not come up with an answer. God forgive me for renouncing you. Yes, I did know God! But not with an intimate relationship! To be honest I had lost contact with him long before I had gotten married.

Does He even know me anymore? He might not recognize me. The devil will do all he can to bring confusion into the equation, and have you question things. I have a broken heart and this big void in my chest. God can't go where sin is and lately that's where I live. The truth of the questions and answers hurt me so bad that I wasn't ready to face the second and third questions. What about my marriage? At 25 years old these were three very hard questions that these strangers asked. They really hit my core, but as I was continually thinking about the questions, the days turned into weeks, and weeks into months. I still haven't made any progress. Do I know God? Am I married? Do you have kids? Yes, I'm married or at least I was. I'm a father of one little girl and expecting another little girl. At 25 this was the first major death I ever faced. I was always known as the class clown and the school's comedian, but after April I had become a sad clown; all at once I lost my smiles and laughter. I didn't know who I was or where I belonged. I always said I would never leave my family! I would never be one of those selfish people! But a reflection in the mirror doesn't lie, I had become one of those people. Then like clockwork my mind was flooded again with those questions. Why did I blame God? Why did I leave my family? Where am I going if I die? Minute by minute hour by hour went by again and before I knew it I was four days in this room still stumbling over three simple questions. After several month's of living in limbo. Living with my wife on and off, living in a fleabag roach motel, staying on different friends' couches and hideaway beds and even a few garage floors. One night a few CMA members found me making my rounds from one dive bar to another dive bar. We visited for a little bit on the street corner and I went on my way. A few days later I came home from work and two of my persistent new friends from the CMA were waiting for me at my apartment. They came upstairs to my empty studio apartment and started telling me about this retreat for men, called Promise Keepers. Promise Keepers, I said I've never heard of it, with an arrogant tone. They said it's a Christian organization for men to help them deal with problems with the help of God. Then I tell them I renounced God. I don't want to hear about this!. I had decided I made my bed. I'm just going to live in it. By now the selfishness that I have inflicted had taken over my whole life.

As my mind is going a hundred miles an hour thinking about everything, but what they're talking about. They finally said you want to go? No, I don't think so, I really don't have the funds to go. Them and God both knew I was lying. I was living in limbo trying to fix my problems. I'll fix my own problems because God has enough to worry about, I often said. I didn't realize God had my name written on the palms of his hands. As in Isaiah 49:16 (NKJV) "See, I have inscribed you on the palms of My hands; Your walls are continually before Me."

I didn't realize God's hands were big enough to handle my mess. As the days went by they kept contacting me over and over. Each time I had to decline. Then finally one day before the event they contacted me and said someone bought a ticket and at the last minute they couldn't go and they requested I took it. Will you accept that gift? I guess so I said. So the four hour drive to Indianapolis seems like it took forever. Each time I was with these people I could really feel a war going on in my soul. It was such an uneasy feeling. I had another famous quote, "If the devil was not bothering you, you may have a problem". Well this day he sure was bothering me. As we pulled into Indianapolis we went to the Hoosier Dome Market Square Stadium, we walked into the entrance and all you could hear was worship music and people screaming and praising God.

I was ready to make a u-turn and head back outside. The group that was with me said, "Oh come on, I think you're going to enjoy this." As we found our seats in this crowded arena that held like 62,000 people. All of a sudden I felt like somebody was ripping me out of my seat. Grown men were crying, shouting and praying to God and the men with me said are you ready to go down to the altar? Um, I said I don't know. It was like an invisible force was pulling me or lifting me out of my chair. I really didn't know much about the Holy Spirit, but as we took the journey down to the center of the arena with hundreds of men around me, I felt like Moses parting the Red Sea. It was amazing how people were just stepping aside as I walked down, not realizing God had a divine appointment; a plan waiting for me just a few steps ahead. Being a shy kid, my head was kind of down the whole time, but I kept walking until I saw a pair of black dress shoes and that's where I stopped. I slowly raised my head to look up and I could have been knocked over with a feather. Standing before me 244 miles from home was the very man I've known my whole life. He was the one that did the funeral services for my departed grandmother just months before. A family friend, a preacher, a man that had helped me out before by giving me a place to live at the Jesus Outreach, when I had no place to stay.

This was the first time in my life that I grabbed a hold of a man and gave him the tightest bear hug I ever could. Something began to happen that I hadn't allowed in several months, I began to weep. As a child I used to tell my grandma real men don't cry and she told me the smallest verse in the Bible is "Jesus wept.", John 11:35 (NKJV). I cried and I cried, and I cried. It seemed like one by one the men left the auditorium floor and it was just me and the preacher, I knew, left there standing in the center. This 62,000 person capacity building was where all the hurt and angerness, hatefulness, the big black hole, the void in my life, the chip on my shoulder all melted away. Let's just take a minute and thank God and praise him. He is so wonderful. "Oh Lord, I thank you for Loving this sinner and never giving up on me. God I thank you. In the blessed name of your son Jesus Christ, I pray. Thank you Lord."

As I was getting ready to part ways with the preacher, he said to me the most profound things. He said, "I've never been hugged by a man so tight and I only live 12 miles from your house. You didn't have to come all the way to Indianapolis to release your anger and seek forgiveness". It is just so wonderful that God always knows what's going on. We act at times when we do something God is surprised, He's not! We need to give him more credit. He knew us before we were formed in our mother's womb. (Jeremiah 1:5 NKJV) He's always two to three steps ahead of us. He knows what's going to happen. I know sometimes it feels like we're alone, but we aren't God is always with us. He's always at your side. He said I will never leave you or forsake you. I will be with you to the end of time. (Hebrews 13:5 NKJV, Deuteronomy 31:6 NKJV, Matthew 28:20 NKJV) What awesome promises.

As I didn't repent that day, I did find peace and mercy in the eyes of God. And He made a way to heal the wounds I had. Sadly the reckless wildlife I loved still was going to be a part of my life for some time to come. From April 1999 to May 11th 2015, I lived wild and carefree. The Bible says "sin is fun for a season" in Hebrews 11:24 (KJV). But after 16 years my season was about to be over!

This testimony you're about to read, kind of fills in the blanks from the beginning of the story:

Sixteen years have passed, I had three children, two daughters and a son, and still a rough and rocky marriage. We were together and apart very often. That's what happens when you enter into matrimony, but don't put God first. My season of sin was no longer fun. Deep down I knew my life wasn't going to last much longer! My life has been a lot of hills and valleys. I grew up at an Assembly of God Church. At age of 15, I had been prophesied over and I was told I had a calling from the Lord to become a Preacher. At the age of 25 my grandmother, the great Pentecostal prayer warrior, had passed away and I renounced God and ran. Boy did I run! I went in and out of Christianity like a leaf tumbling in a whirlwind. I just couldn't stay, I always felt the urge to keep running; like Jonah running from God. I always felt a great connection with Jonah. Even before I could read that was always my favorite Bible story. My grandmother read it to me several times a day. I'm sure she got tired of it at times; the things we do out of love. Well, my 16 year season of sinful living was prescription drugs, sneaking around with other women, and drowning my problems in a bottle. I had tried it all. Picking up women on the street instead of my children, to running my Harley as fast as I could while under the influence of sin and narcotics.

Finally, in 2015 my season of fun came to an end. There were many signs along the way that God was giving me one last chance to turn from my evil ways. The lifestyle I had once loved was beginning to wear me down. There were husbands after me because of the affairs with their wives. My best friend was depression, I was eating pills to sleep and eating pills to wake up. My life was spinning out of control. I felt so low and down in despair that I felt the devil had to look down to see me. I learned alot my about my so-called friends (AKA Fake friends), they are hard to find when they hear and discover that you're down. Through my journey I noticed who my real friends were; it wasn't the ones that scattered like roaches when I needed help or when I had fallen into despair. How great of a friend I was when the booze and the pills were accessible, but when the partying was no longer fun my fair weather friends left my side faster than a person hits the brakes when they see a cop.

My oldest daughter went off to college and it just broke my already cracked up heart. My father's health was failing, our house caught fire and burned to the ground. We lost everything! My daughter came home from college with the news that she dropped out and was pregnant. I didn't handle it very well, I really went off the deep end and blew my top, by disgracing her and running her down and by telling her how she had ruined her life. I told her she needed to get an abortion or put it up for adoption because at age 41 I'm not going to be a grandfather. Oh my what else can go wrong? Sometimes I feel the almighty allows things to happen to us as for us to stop and open up our eyes.

On May 11, 2015, Mother's day night, my daughter, Tanisha Jo, came to me and said, "Dad the baby hasn't kicked, can you take me to the hospital?" As I still hadn't made peace with her pregnancy, but being concerned we hurried to the hospital. On the way to the hospital I made a very bad joke about something that had happened to me when I was a baby. My mother lost a lot of blood during her C-section and the cord was wrapped around my neck and the doctor told my dad and my great grandfather one of us would live and one of us would surely die. The doctor told him he might have to choose which one would live. Praise God we both lived, but as a joke, I asked my daughter if something went wrong who were we to choose, her or the baby, ha ha. Who knew that it might have come down to having to make that decision.

We got up to the labor and delivery floor of the hospital and were the only family up there and they put Tanisha in a room. Tanisha was given shots to try and stop labor because she still had six weeks to go. Instead of the shots stopping labor, they caused the baby to relax and they lost the baby's heartbeat. Tanisha's blood pressure had dropped immensely and there was no sign of life with the baby. It became pandemonium on that Mother's day weekend on the OB floor. All of sudden, wires were getting unplugged, things were getting knocked over, people were being pushed out of the way to get mother and baby prepared for an emergency C-section. They took my wife to get gowned up and go in there with her to sign papers and calm Tanisha. Once Tanisha was settled, my wife came out and went to call family members to inform them of what was going on. As I stood all alone in the hallway wondering what just happened; the phone at the nurse's station rang and the charge nurse answered the phone. I was only a few feet away to hear the nurse say, "The mother made it, but the baby had died". All of a sudden I felt something for a child that I had not felt before. I couldn't fathom what was going on. The doors opened up at the other end of the hallway, it was another nurse and before she could say anything to me, I said "Where is the chapel?" She gave me the directions.

Once my wife came back, I told her I would be right back and I literally ran as fast as I could down the hospital corridor looking for the chapel. Living the life of a hoodlum, it was truly an invitation from the Lord to bring back to my memory to always seek him; and in this very dark time I was doing just that seeking, looking, and searching for the Lord.

As I got to the entrance of the chapel, I immediately fell to my knees and prayed. My face was buried in the carpet, my face hit the carpet before my feet did. Then I began to pray this prayer, "Jesus please take my life and send me into the deepest part of the lake of fire. I surrender up my soul so this child may have an opportunity to live. I am a worthless sinner. I am no good inside or out or to anyone." As I wept, with my face on this rough carpet, I made one final plea. With a deep breath I said, "Heavenly Father in the name of your son Jesus Christ, if you allow this baby to live I will worship and serve you until my last breath here on earth. Amen."

As I began to wipe away the tremendous amount of tears that had fallen from my bloodshot eyes; I erected to my feet and tried to get my composure and straighten myself up. Kind of get a sobering look to me so it didn't look like I had been crying. I felt like I had been on my knees for hours. As I began the journey of walking back down the endless lonesome hospital corridor I was rehearsing in my mind and trying to figure out what to say to break the sad news to my wife. How to tell her that our first grandchild has passed away. It felt like I was walking forever to get back to the OB department.

As I came to the automatic ob doors the tears were coming back. The doors swung open and there was my wife and a few different family members. I felt the apple size lump in my throat. As I began to utter the words "Ter", before I could get the words Terrie Kay out, she said to me, "WHERE HAVE YOU BEEN?" Come over here and look at your granddaughter, Amelia Rae! What? He heard me! She was born six weeks early 18.5 ft long, no physical or mental defects, a perfect healthy baby girl. Mother and baby went home three days later.

I definitely have to argue with people when they say God doesn't perform miracles. I have a testimony; that five year old girl's doing great and she started kindergarten this year (Aug 2020). God is awesome.

That very next Sunday, I went to church and gave my testimony and then I proudly walked twenty steps to the altar to rededicate my life and fulfill my promise to the Lord. At 41 years old, I gave my life to Christ. My wife Terrie Kay, my middle daughter Taylor Ann, and her friend all got saved that Sunday morning in May. Thank you Lord for not tossing up your hands and sending me to the depths of hell for the wild life I led. I know you had ample opportunity and reason to do so. Thank you again Lord.

My brothers and sisters let me tell you when I accepted Christ into my life it was 10,000 times greater than any trip I had ever been on.

God is awesome

Sincerely,
Billy Davison

After Receiving Christ

What happened after I gave my life back to Christ? Oh it has been a very interesting series of events. Not long after those twenty steps to the altar, I decided to be rebaptized and rededicate my life to Christ. "And he said unto them, Go ye into all the world, and preach the gospel to every creature." Mark 16:15 (NKJV) About six months after I received Jesus Christ back into my life. I was rebaptized into the Holy Spirit down in the flooded Illinois River town of Liverpool, Illinois.

A small river community of less than 100 people, I'm guessing. I couldn't tell you if anyone again has been baptized down in that muddy, murky, dark water of the Illinois River or not, but it was a very nice Sunday summer day, and about thirty family and friends of the church came to witness this Holy event. There was a catfish tournament going on and the fisherman were getting cranky as they were putting boats in and out on the flooded banks, where excited Christians were in their way worshiping the Lord and singing songs upon the levee.

When God wants to get people's attention He sure knows how, and that day He did for sure. "And do not fear those who kill the body but cannot kill the soul. But rather fear Him who is able to destroy both soul and body in hell.", Matthew 10:28 (NKJV). There were four of us that day standing in front of the whole world confessing that we gave our lives to Jesus Christ. Myself, my wife, my middle daughter, and someone from another church all were Baptized. I went down first, I remember coming out of the water thinking I was to see the clouds move and hear God speak. He didn't, but He already had things in motion! Again it shows you we are always on His mind. Something I'm sure you'll realize after reading these testimonies. God never misses a beat! And what he had in store - it showed the following Sunday.

The church invited a guest speaker, Tom, who came to our little river town, country church. He was working in the gifts of prophecy, words of knowledge, and healing, that were taking place in that little church. To my amazement something wonderful was getting ready to happen to me. Something else that was going to change my life.

I was standing up in front of the church, just to catch anyone that got slayed in the Spirit. As I stood behind this young lady with my hands ready to catch her when she fell, all of the sudden the amazing power of the Holy Spirit went through her and right into me. It felt like an unharnessed electricity went into me. I, myself, had received these miraculous gifts, I now have. I was filled with an overflowing power of the Holy Spirit, such as speaking in tongues, as recorded in the book of Acts, and also the gift of healing and knowledge, recorded in 1 Corinthians 12.

FEBRUARY 10, 2019

"I, Billy Davison, being a servant of Jesus Christ. Over three years now, I have seen miraculous healings and I have given great testimonies of the awesome power of Jesus Christ. The Lord put on my heart to write this. To give witness of how HE has had his hand on my life since I was born. My grandmother was a great woman of faith, she always lifted me and others up in prayer. I thank Jesus Christ for her. As I grow closer to the 50-year mark, I am saddened that she was such a great woman of God and I didn't learn more from her. She had a vast knowledge of the word of God. She was truly a mighty prayer warrior of the day. On January 26, 1974, and almost died. My mother had lost a lot of blood and the umbilical cord was wrapped around my neck. My father always told me that the doctors came to him and said you might have to decide who will live and who won't. My mother was really weak, but praise the lord we both got through. That was the very first recollection of the healing hand of God, I was told about. I now know the power of the Holy Spirit was in my life. At the age of five, because of sin, my sister and I were regrettably left at a park by the mighty Spoon River. Again, only by the grace of God were we protected and kept safe. A five year old boy and a three year old girl could have wandered down to the river or been abducted, but praise God we never were. Again, I just want to praise God and thank him for the great works he's done in my entire life. I love you Jesus.

In the winter of 1983, I was helping my dad, while he was servicing his semi. I remember it was bitterly cold and I was sitting right beside the wood stove that he was trying to light. I remember like it was yesterday, I was sitting on a semi tire right beside the door of the stove playing with a toy semi and trailer, when all of a sudden there was a backdraft and the stove exploded. Dad and I we're on fire, physically. Being a young kid my first instinct was to run, so I ran out of the shop toward the creek in the back of the property; with the flame burning me and my dad screaming drop and roll. Miraculously the fire went out. Again only by the power of God I'm still here. We were rushed to the hospital. I had singed hair and my clothes were burnt to me. Praise God, my hospital visit was short and I had very minor burns. As I'm sitting here writing this and reminiscing about my life, I know for certain we have guardian angels sent from God. You know everyone in the world has experienced some kind of an invitation from God. A form of protection they might never even have thought about.

As I sit here writing this testimony so many close calls keep popping up. One thing is almost being run over by a tractor that was rolling out of control; which I could have been killed, but somehow I was able to safely jump on this runaway tractor and get it stopped.

As I look back it's hard to believe that I did not get run over and smashed. I was only about twelve years old and it was only the work of God that kept me safe. When I was sixteen years old, my friend and I decided to take a canoe, no paddles, but a tape player, and put it in a flooded creek. The water had to be eleven or twelve feet deep and the currant was moving thirty or forty miles an hour.

How didn't we capsize and drown; because Jesus and his angels were in that boat with us, that's the only explanation I have. I mean two foolish teenage boys in a canoe. Most likely we were intoxicated, it should have been a certainty that we drowned. Again you have got to admit Jesus had our lives in his hand and protected us. I don't think I ever said it, but thank you Lord for keeping us safe.

Just a year later, at seventeen years old my girlfriend (who would become my wife) was taking me back home in her pickup truck and she hit loose gravel and the truck rolled. My passenger door couldn't open and the top of the truck was smashed down. We landed back on all four tires, but the driver's door was the only one able to open. We should have been killed, but again we survived with minor scratches and bruises. It was pointed out later about the shirt I was wearing, I believe it said "Trust in God".

I know it was God who has protected me my entire life. My junior year of high school I broke into a gas station that was recently abandoned, because I heard some seniors getting ready to do it that night. They had dug a tunnel, so I thought during lunch I would beat them to the punch. I didn't steal anything or take anything out of it, but I did break into it and that allowed a lot of people to go in and take what they wanted. The cops came to the high school and arrested me. The very same day another one of the chains of gas stations that was abandoned had the same thing happen to them. This is where I know prayer really works. That kid went to prison for ten years, I just got my hand slapped; no probation, no fines, nothing, but to keep my nose clean. That really was the work of God, and I knew it.

By May 1993, I finally was eligible to graduate high school. The day before graduation my guidance counselor, who had to come to know me and my grandmother very well, because of my honryness; called me into his office and said, "You need to thank your grandma because if it wasn't for the fact of her being a mighty prayer warrior there is no way in this world you would graduate". God is truly on your side he said, looking back I must agree.

In 1998, I wrecked my semi by the pictures and the accident report I should have been killed instantly. Again, I came out of it with scratches and a few bruises. By reading this you have to admit God has great plans for my life. If you have read my other testimonies you know I was a very big heathen and I ran from God a lot, but he has always been there to protect me. Even when I wasn't faithful to him. It is true, what a great and wonderful God we serve. As I close I want to tell you Jesus Christ is the greatest high I have ever been on. I am here to tell you after living in sin and the world for twenty years, and living for Christ for four years; finding Christ was the greatest thing I have ever done. I have prospered in every area of my life. The only thing I regret is not going to Christ sooner. He truly is my savior. God bless you. Billy Davison"

I have been lucky enough to witness hundreds of awesome moves of the Lord in people's lives. As a truck driver I had the chance to minister and lead people to Christ, that didn't even know him. The Lord made a way for me to be able to pick up Bibles from different locations and places and give them to the lost and those that were new brothers and sisters in Christ. Some of these people have never even read the magnificent word of the Lord. I just praise the Lord and continually thank HIM for opening the doors to help me get Bibles and take them in places that many can't.

The Bible donations itself is a very great testimony of how great and wonderful God is and how he works in mysterious ways. I have seen several healings and had numerous words of knowledge since the Lord put this great anointing on my life and I want to share a few stories with you.

Before I start, I want to say I am nothing without Jesus Christ. I am just a tool, a pencil in the hand of the almighty God. After being saved and anointed I prayed earnestly for a year for Jesus to send someone to my path and teach me how to truly work, move and operate in these gifts. And the answer to my prayer came after one Sunday morning service. This reformed Holy Spirit-filled former Southern Baptist preacher, named Michael Floyd, approached me and said I would like for you to come to my house.

That divine appointment by God started an avalanche of a wonderful and tremendous teaching and healing Ministry. And a golden friendship that still holds a very special place in my heart, even this very hour. Apart or together the Holy Spirit has done awesome works with us. The Lord has made a wonderful team out of Mike and myself. I thank the Lord daily for Mike and his wife. They truly were a God sent. I cannot thank God enough for sending him to me. He has taught me so much that I would have never known without him. He's responsible for helping me talk to the congregation and helping me with being a shy introvert. Thank you Lord for this great man of God. I am just a little better man for having had him in my life, and teaching me all the wonderful things the word of God says. I will always be indebted to them for all the help they have given my family and I. Thank you Brother and sister Floyd. You'll never be forgotten.

You were always so patient and kind to me, and when I would need to be corrected you did it out of love. You gave me a glimpse into a world of love. Because of your great obedience, my personal Ministry has been made possible. I don't think you'll ever truly understand the great doors that were open because you took me under your wings and took the time to teach me what others wouldn't! Wherever you go in the world, if I could, I would tag along. If I never see you again I know we'll walk together one day in Glory. When the Holy Spirit told me to write this book I said, "Lord

I need someone fantastic and special to write the forward and the Holy Spirit said have Mike do it". As I thought about asking him I said, "Wow, Lord you're right there is nobody better fitted and more qualified. He is a perfect choice".

It was a true honor to have my friend, my brother, my mentor and my professor Pastor Michael Floyd begin this book just as he helped begin my Ministry. It kind of came full circle. I know King David was a man after God's Own Heart and I believe with my whole heart and my whole being, so is Pastor Mike Floyd. Below is the first meeting I went to and was introduced by this pastor, my great friend Michael Floyd.

JENNIFER'S STORY

Now this was an interesting story because this is one of my first experiences with the gifts of healing and the word of knowledge, as I can recall of her story.

In her early forties she found out she had cancer. She would have battled it for five years and by the time I had met her it had become a progressive stage four brain cancer. And all hope was lost and the doctor said there was nothing more they could do for her so she needed to go live her life. Now, who knows that what doctors say and God says are two different things at times. Who knows that faith is an action word. So you must do something to make your faith work.

It all started with that late Autumn evening. It was a cool night in 2018, in a small rural area in Western Illinois. Terrie Kay and I were invited to accompany Pastor Floyd and his wife to a tent revival meeting in Western Illinois. Many awesome things happened that night, but I want to focus on this story for right now.

When I get a word of knowledge about somebody that's having a pain in their body or any physical or emotional issue; I also feel that physical and emotional pain. Tonight I was being blessed with it all. As soon as the Revival started so did the movement of the Holy Spirit. Who knows God said, "I will never leave you or forsake you", in Deuteronomy 31:6 NKJV, And, "I will be with you until the end of time" in Matthew 28:20 NKJV.

I was getting much discomfort from a massive migraine, one I've never experienced in my life. A headache so bad that I literally wanted to cry. If we had driven ourselves I would have gone home. It hurt that bad. We were the last speakers of the night. As we got up I kind of hid behind Pastor Mike, and being a shy kid I couldn't speak so I would write each word on a post-it and hand it to him. Pastor Mike asked if anyone had a bad headache. I peeked around his side and spoke up and said the headache is so severe I want to cry myself, so I imagine they are in awful pain.

All of a sudden this young woman and her husband headed up toward us. She was using a walker so I wasn't sure what was going on. As she finally reached the front of the podium, I said ma'am are you having a headache? With tears streaming down her weather-beaten face she said, "Oh yes". Her husband said that she struggles with headaches all day long because she has stage four brain cancer. He then explained that the doctor said they couldn't do anything else for her. With that said I stepped out from behind Mike and I said, "I rebuke that in the name of Jesus Christ!" And then I prayed for her. As Mike and I and the congregation stood around her in a circle and laid hands on her and I prayed life over her and commanded in the name of Jesus Christ that the pain be gone from her.

The headache went immediately off of me and she was excited and said her headache was gone. I smiled and said that's great and she said, you don't understand, it's constant, it never leaves and it's totally gone. That night she accepted her healing from cancer. A few weeks later I received a social media message from her that she had gone to the doctor and there is no sign of cancer in her body. She said you healed me! I said I did nothing, but laid my dirty hands on you. God healed you. Give him all the praise and thanks. God is the great physician. He doesn't want us to be sick or suffer he wants us to be well and live prosperous and healthy. Praise the Lord she was healed!!

There were many great healings that night. Another I would like to share with you is a story of a broken heart. This was a first for me. After Jennifer received her healing I got a word and all the sudden a sorrow overcame me, a broken heart exclaimed. It was a minister whose wife had just passed away. He was really surprised that I knew that since we were strangers. I said I knew it had to be somebody close because I had the same feeling I had when my father had passed away. So we prayed for him; for peace and comfort during his mourning. After the service was over we were asked if we wanted to go inside the house and have dinner, which was prepared for us traveling evangelists. During that time we continued to fellowship and the pastor who was in mourning started asking me questions about my gifts and how all of a sudden the Holy Spirit gives me a word. I laughed and said the Lord also told me you have left knee pain and he just looked stunned. He said 30 years ago he was cutting wood and tripped and ripped the cartilage in his knee and he's had several surgeries and they still can't correct it. I asked if I could pray for him. I got on my knees and as soon as I put my hand on his knee the Holy Spirit miraculously healed him!

He said my knee is hot. I said praise God you have been healed!! Glory Hallelujah. After that great healing I was able to talk to him about the gifts which he never understood, but after that night that pastor's Church was going to be different. There were many more words. I believe ten total words and ten healings not bad for an attendance that was around thirteen people.

This was a great experience for me and all who attended. The Holy Spirit is a fantastic teacher! If we are faithful and follow him where he sends us he will always be there to help us. It's all about obedience. All the thanks goes to the Lord. It's not me who does these wonderful works, but the Lord! I am nothing without him. Since the Lord has anointed me in these past years I have seen awesome things. I truly believe God has a great sense of humor because as we were leaving that night a lady said I'm surprised you didn't have words for me. I said what was your problem? She said oh

I have a severe toothache. I said actually I wrote that down on my post-it and I showed her. I touched her forehead and said toothache be gone. she immediately was slain in the spirit and slid down the counter where she stood and people just laughed as she lay there. I said I bet she won't say anything again. I said a blessing over her as I parted their company and walked into the cool night air. God is awesome.

TERRIE KAY'S STORY

"I was having pain in my hips and lower back, which I knew I had arthritis in my lower back. I had fallen walking out of our camper around 2010 and had been hurting off and on ever since. When we became grandparents, I told Billy how upsetting it was that I wasn't going to be able to get on the floor and play with my grandkids. It hurt too bad to get down on the floor and I wouldn't be able to get back up off the floor. Then one day Billy came to me and told me to sit down and hold my legs up. I thought what in the world are you doing? He told me he thought he knew why I was in so much pain, so I sat down and lifted both legs up. One leg was shorter than the other. Billy had just been watching a video with Todd White. On the video Todd prayed over a person and their leg grew out. So Billy prayed over my legs and my leg grew out an inch or two. Once my legs were even I stood up and moved around, in ways that hurt before. I felt no pain and I have been crawling around on the floor and tormenting my grandchildren ever since the oldest turned one in May of 2016. Thank you Lord for fixing my leg and getting rid of the pain. Thank you Billy for listening to God and letting him use you as a tool to heal others. The Lord has blessed me and my family in so many ways. This was just one of the many blessings from God. Thank you Lord." Terrie Kay Davison

God Isn't Ready For You To Come Home Just Yet

I 've got two great deathbed stories. The first one was in a nursing home. The Holy Spirit put on my heart to go visit a relative in a certain nursing home. It just happened that my daughter worked there at the time and she met me at the entrance and walked with me to my great uncle's room. As I walked past one of the rooms along the corridor a sorrow hit me and I had such a heartache that I grabbed my chest. My daughter literally thought I was having a heart attack. She said, Are you okay? I said, I'm not sure, I'm not sure what's going on here. This was a first for me, so I just kept on walking and the further I got away from the room the feeling went off of me. This incident was only a few weeks after I got this anointing. I wasn't really sure what it was. I visited with my uncle and shared Jesus with him. I told him Jesus is right here beside you and he chuckled and said I knew he was in here somewhere. I come from a long line of family members with an awesome sense of humor. After visiting with my great-uncle, Tanisha Jo and I were heading back down the hallway toward the exit when I came to that room again and the symptoms hit me even harder than before this time. I looked into the room as I walked by wondering what was going on. The physical and emotional experience I was going through was hitting me so bad you could literally see it on my face this time.

Tanisha grabbed my arm and with a concerned look on her face said, "Dad are you okay? Do I need to get a nurse?" I said no I believe someone in here needs to be prayed for.

As she was walking me outside she asked me if I noticed the cart outside that room and I said no. She said it is a courtesy cart. I Inquired further about what that was and she said when a resident of the nursing home is passing away they make up something for the family. I had never heard of that, but I thought what an awesome thing to do. As I walked to my car, with tears in my eyes the Holy Spirit told me to pray. So I got in my car and dropped my head on the steering wheel and I prayed and cried for 45 minutes for the family that was saying their last goodbyes.

A few days later I asked my daughter about the person in the room with the courtesy cart and how they were doing. She said, "Dad you won't believe it". It was a miracle the individual didn't die, all the sudden she got 100% better and is out of harm's way. The awesome part of this story is it was Palm Sunday. All I can say is praise the Lord for another awesome miracle.

Now this second deathbed story shows that God puts us right where we're needed at the very exact time he wants to use us. He is such an awesome God.

DIVINE APPOINTMENTS WITH GOD

This next testimony is about a woman named Donna. This story is how God will use us wherever we are. In March 2017 I was at a Bible study and my wife came in abruptly and whispered in my ear your family needs you at the hospital, you have an uncle that's not doing good and he's asking for you. It is so awesome how things work out and what God has planned. As I arrived at the hospital, I walked in the doors and I was ushered right to my uncle's room; and I was being updated by family members that his health was deteriorating fast and it was just a matter of hours before he left this earth. As I walked into the entrance of his hospital room two different family members ran up to me and kissed me and thanked me for coming to say goodbye. Immediately I rebuked the situation and I started praying life over my uncle. People don't understand it's not God's will for us to be sick. 1 Peter 2:24 (NKJV) tells us that "by His stripes we were healed". It doesn't say we might be healed or that we could be healed. It says we WERE, past-tense, healed.

As I joined hands around his hospital bed, I stood on the word of God and prayed for life over him. I loved on him, shared stories with him, and continued to tell him he would live. I told him I will see you later and I exited his room knowing he was healed and he would live to see many days ahead. I decided to go outside and get some fresh air and visit with some cousins. As I was standing outside visiting, this car pulled up to the entrance to the ER, where I was standing. And this lady was being helped out of her car. She looked like she was in agonizing pain and I heard the Holy Spirit say go pray for her, but being kind of shy and thinking what will my family's number say Or think, I wasn't being very obedient to do exactly what the Holy Spirit said. I just stood there knowing I'm letting God down!

As I walked back into the hospital, I noticed that family was being checked in at the desk. I needed some alone time because the guilt was too much to bear; the guilt of not listening to the Holy Spirit. I headed upstairs and I locked myself in a bathroom and prayed, cried, and repented for not being obedient. When God tells you to do something and you don't, the feeling you have of shame and let down and just being totally disappointed with yourself, is much worse than not being obedient. Oftentimes we listen more to our flesh than to God, look at Jonah.

As I went back down to join my family in the waiting room and give them some words of encouragement before heading home; I noticed that the lady and her family were sitting there patiently waiting for someone to call her back to the examination room. I thought Lord, I know them. As I departed, yes I had another chance to minister to her and guess what? UGH!!! I dislike being shy. It's something I have to work on daily. It's hard to be obedient when I live under this curse of shyness. Lord please help me with it.

As i was driving home the Lord just kept putting that lady on my heart. I said, "Lord please bring back to my remembrance how I know them". So when I got home I immediately got on my computer, on social media and found her children and sent them a message that said this, "Hi this might sound weird, but I felt like the Holy Spirit wanted me to lay hands on your mom and pray, but she looked like she was in so much pain. Since I didn't really know her I couldn't take that step of obedience. Please know she's in my prayers." That night the response I got back was we're not really religious and there's a lot we don't know, but thank you. I prayed all night. I talked to the daughter about Christ, and found out the mother was doing better, but she was still not out of the woods. I kept sharing Jesus Christ with Megan, her daughter. I kept encouraging her to give these problems to Christ during the next few weeks. As I was ministering to her and praying for her mother, she ended up giving her life to Christ. Now in the next few months the mother got well, but then got sick, then well, and then sick again.

Then one night I was coming home off the road in my semi and as I passed her house the Holy Spirit said STOP. I said Lord I can't, I have a 80,000 lb truck and no place to park it along this highway. So I headed home and called Megan. She said frantically, "Billy we need you. It's bad". Well, I had no other transportation, so I had to wait for my wife and daughter to get home from a school ball game. I felt in my heart that it may be too late. That hour-and-a-half wait seemed like forever, but it finally came and the three of us hightailed it over to this house to pray.

As soon as we walked in the house it was so cold and gloomy. I immediately started blessing the house and rebuking any Spirit of Infirmity. As we walked back to this corner bedroom, Megan's mom, Donna, was laying in bed under several layers of blankets. My daughter and wife thought she had passed. I knew she hadn't, but in my heart I knew she wouldn't last much longer. So I immediately dropped to my knees and touched her ankle and began to pray. I prayed with every ounce of energy I had. I prayed life over her, I rebuked death, I rebuked the devil, I rebuked every sickness and infirmity that was holding her hostage in her body. I evicted the devil, and in the name of Jesus I stood firm on his word and his authority. I saw her healed on a deathbed. I felt a warmth on her leg that just moments before was cold as ice. As soon as I said Amen I felt a great peace come through the whole house and I walked down the hallway and touched every wall and every doorway. Hand-rubbed oil on it and prayed for a hedge of protection and the blood of the lamb over everything under that roof and blessed Megan with a prayer and then headed home.

On our way home Terrie Kay and Taylor Ann we're talking about this experience. They were asking many questions, they said they thought she had died and we were praying over a dead body. I said, if we hadn't intervened and been obedient to God she would've been. She was Just minutes from passing away. I said that's why I was saying how crucial it was we got over there and why I was so aggravated I had no car and I had to wait. I've noticed in my Ministry when me and my wife knock heads and start to argue a lot something awesome is about ready to happen for the kingdom of God and the devil is doing all he can to stop it by putting up barricades and roadblocks and drama. He does this to stop God's plan, but who knows that the tools the devil uses to tear us down God will use to build us up!

Eight o'clock the next morning I was awakened by my cell phone blowing up. I had several messages on my phone to please call Donna's house. I grabbed my Bible, went into my office, prayed and then called. I don't even think the phone rang and I could hear the excitement on the other end. Music playing and Megan eagerly shouting excitingly, "My MOM is up and cooking breakfast. She's singing, Dancing She's full of joy. She hasn't been able to do this for quite a while". I said, that's awesome. Isn't God great. She said as soon as I laid my hand on her mom's leg her mom felt a heat and a love and joy came upon her. I said, praise the Lord that was the Holy Spirit Breaking the shackles of death off of her. Weeks later Donna accepted Jesus Christ as her personal savior.

FOLLOWING ARE TESTIMONIES FROM MEGAN AND DONNA.

"Hello my name is Megan, I have known Billy since I was probably a 7th grader (I'm 43 now lol) so a long time. We were two very different people than we are nowadays. I first saw Billy and his wife Terrie in the hospital parking lot when I had taken my mom into the emergency room for complications from scar tissue, intestinal blockages, and diverticulitis. He was up there for his family's emergency visit. As hours and days went by, my mom got worse and had to have surgery that was supposed to be a two hour surgery but lasted well over five hours. When she came out of surgery the dr informed us she would need to be in extended care and was on a ventilator. Immediately my heart sank and I told the dr she would be coming home and I would take care of her. I went to be with her in the ICU and prayed harder and more than I've ever prayed before. I put more faith in God than I ever have in my life. Billy messaged me out of the blue and him and his wife Terrie prayed for my mom and I and also prayed with me. I begged God to please allow my mom to stay with us and get better. Billy never left my side that entire night. He prayed and prayed to no end. This all took place over Facebook messenger. My mom kept coming to a little bit, unable to talk due to the vent, but begging me with her eyes to help her. The fear in her eyes broke my heart. She kept struggling to ask me if she was dying. I reassured her she was not all while pleading with God in my mind to please save her. As I laid my head on the side of my mom's bed, holding her hand, begging God to give my mom comfort and rest and healing, all of the sudden, with my eyes closed, I saw the brightest, most golden light I have ever seen. It was almost like the direct sunlight was shining so very bright right in my moms ICU room; however, the brightest sun I have ever seen. Immediately I knew it was God shining on my mom. The Dr assured us that my mom would be taken off of the vent in the morning once the anesthesia wore off. After God visited my mom's room she started to rest more peacefully, she wasn't waking as much with the terrified look in her eyes, and she started to take more breaths on her own. It was just a matter of a couple more hours and the Dr was able to take the ventilator off of her which was about 2-4 hours sooner than expected. She improved quite quickly after that and was released to go home with me as her caretaker within a few days. As the days passed, my mom wasn't feeling herself and didn't seem to be improving as expected. Please keep in mind, Billy and I stayed in close contact after we were home and he continued to pray for us and offer us guidance in trusting in the Lord. My mom ended up back in the hospital with four abscesses that required more surgery. It was flu season and all hospitals were full within a 70 mile radius. No hospital or Dr would accept her. Graham Hospital was just letting her lay and get sicker. It took me begging hospitals and Drs and having a discussion with the hospital board and having to really jump through hoops for three days before I was able to get my mom transferred by ambulance to Proctor. They immediately did surgery to put in drain tubes for the abscesses. Billy stayed in contact and constant communication and prayer with us. Since he's a truck driver he couldn't make it back in time to get to Peoria. He contacted a friend of his to come to the hospital to pray for my mom, but by the time they got there my mom was back in the ambulance and headed back to Graham Hospital. There were days spent in the hospital, days at home, days back at the hospital and back and forth for a couple months. My mom was wearing down. She was done mentally, physically and emotionally. I was determined to help my mom get better and I was relying on God and Billy to help me do that. My mom continued to deteriorate and I was losing hope as to how I could help her. I was doing all I could, but it wasn't enough. I couldn't help her as her health was failing her. I messaged Billy and asked him if he would pray for my mom, that she was failing and I was afraid she was getting worse. He immediately asked if him and his wife could come over to pray over my mom. As far as I was concerned, he couldn't get there fast enough. Billy, his wife and their daughter, Taylor, came over. He touched my moms leg, and his wife held my hand as I held my little boy and we stood and prayed. My mom was so weak and was giving up. I bet it wasn't three days later that my mom had major improvements and just continued to improve from there. To this day she keeps up with all day running scavenger hunts with me from piecing together Halloween costumes for my little boy and I, or just running errands or taking little day trips to enjoy some sun and fun. Billy directed us to His River of Life Church where we met the most wonderful church family. They welcomed us with open arms and taught us the ways of God. We both got baptized by Pastor Sheldon and it felt so good to be saved and give my life to God. I fail God daily, so many times, but not a minute goes by that I don't thank him for my life with my little boy and my mom. I'm so grateful for both of them and I will always put my faith and trust in Him to keep them, and myself healthy, happy and safe.

I must add more. I was at one of the lowest points in my life with personal family issues that I cannot go into great detail about due to the safety of my little boy and myself. However, I can say that putting trust in man to save and protect is not always the best answer. Although, it is easy to be fooled into thinking higher order people have others' best interest at heart. As usual, Billy and I had been in contact as he counseled me on God and how to trust in Him and how to hand it all over to Him. I was struggling with so many things. I did my best to allow God to take over the situation and the people involved. I tried my best to trust in Him and have faith above all and everyone else, that He would save and protect us. Mind you, me doing and trying my best to relinquish that type of "control" was not easy and I look back now and even though I did, I sure didn't very much. not like I do nowadays anyway. I was facing some very big and win all or lose all battles and even against the devil himself, the battles were won. They weren't won 100% but they were won enough that I will forever be grateful. I remember talking to Billy right before one of the big meetings and he prayed and before I quit talking to him he said give it to God, let Him guide you and your truths. I again cannot go into detail at this time but I can say that the exact meeting I'm referring to saved what was at stake. If it hadn't been for Billy and his guidance and consistent counsel then I wouldn't have found God and put my trust in Him. I wouldn't have known to trust His guidance and put my faith in Him and not man.

Life is still just as crazy (chaos) and wild (heartbreaking) as it was before but I deal with it differently and I know God makes that possible. He gives me strength, he gives me guidance and he preserves me daily. Without Him, I honestly don't know how I would be dealing with all of the things I am forced to face. But with Him, I know I will and we will be just fine."

"Hello my name is Donna, Almost 3 years ago I was very sick. I have always been a strong person, but I had been sick for a very long time. I came home from the hospital from my second surgery in a year. I tried to get better. My oldest daughter and husband were helping me do everything; I couldn't even bathe myself, couldn't stand to cook, do dishes, and was in constant pain. I prayed to God to please help me. After several days I made my peace with God I prayed that I was tired and my family would be better off without me. I felt like I was a burden. That night I prayed to God to take me. My daughter Megan came into my room as I was drifting off to sleep and asked if it was ok if Billy could come and lay hands on me and pray over me. I said ok cause I really didn't think I would be here the next morning. He told Megan he drove by our house in his semi and God told him he would stop here. So Billy, his wife Terrie and daughter Taylor came into my room and he laid his hand on my ankle and he began to pray. I remember the warmth of his hand and the presence of Megan, Terrie, and Taylor & Billy. As he prayed

I could fill my whole body getting warm and I was thinking I'm finally warm and I went to sleep. When I awoke the next morning I was surprised I was warm, I felt pretty good, I fixed breakfast. I hadn't done that in a long time. I could actually feel myself healing. God has given Billy a gift and to this day I can fill the pressure and the warmth on my ankle where Billy had his hand praying for my life. Thank you God for giving Billy such a wonderful gift. And thank you Billy for putting the Lord back into my life. And thank you Terrie & Taylor for coming and giving Megan support thru my most desperate time. Love you guys And thank you."

THE NEXT TESTIMONY IS ABOUT MARGE

This story is a very awesome lesson about being obedient. It all started one beautiful summer afternoon. I was sitting on my porch enjoying the sunshine and the summertime heat, rocking away in my favorite chair while reading the Bible. When all the sudden the Holy Spirit said go pray for Marge. I thought, WHAT. I haven't seen her for twenty years and I was a kind of a heathen and I don't think she even likes me! But again the Holy Spirit said, "Go lay hands on her so she can be healed". I had seen on social media that she had been battling cancer and she was giving up. I don't know what it is about human nature, but when God tells us to do something, the first thing we do is question it.

A great example is in the book of Jonah. God tells Jonah to do something and he does the opposite. So after the Holy Spirit said go pray for her, I tried to make a deal. Well, if you bring her to me or she calls me or this or that I'll do it, but there was no response. So I put on my shoes and started walking around Marge's residence. She lives in a huge apartment complex and I didn't even know what room she lived in. I said that's okay Lord she'll see me walking around and yell for me. I did a lap or two and nothing, so I went home. I said, "Well Lord I tried" and nothing was said by Him, but I was getting convicted bad. So I tried to find her on social media, but it didn't work. I waited for a few more hours and I contacted her son, a boyhood friend of mine. I told him I was trying to get a hold of his mom and could he please tell me how to reach her.

This tug-of-war with God lasted almost eight hours. Once I denied self and did what the Lord told me, I knew amazing things were going to happen. The next morning Marge contacted me through social media and I said I'd like to come pray for you, will that be okay? Like I said the last time she saw me I was a Harley Davidson riding heathen. So I could only imagine her first thought, but she gracefully agreed and invited me over. I went in the back entrance and when I saw her my heart broke. I saw this elderly lady sitting there with a walker and frail looking. If I could guess I bet she weighed 60 lbs, no hair, and very weak. I asked if we could go somewhere private to talk and as we followed her into another room I prayed, "Lord this is all you what? Am I supposed to tell her immediately?" God said, "Unforgiveness".

As we were sitting down, I just stared at her. Her skin looked like thin paper and I said, "Marge, let me tell you how I found God". After we all had a good cry, of how great God was and how he rescued me and resurrected my Granddaughter, I told her that God wanted to heal her, but you have unforgiveness. I read a scripture in Mark. Mark 11:24-26 (NKJV), which says that God cannot forgive us if we cannot forgive others. I said, I hope you understand who this word is about and immediately she started crying. She said it was unforgiveness for her daughter that had passed away. I told her that God said just forgive her right now and you'll be healed.

I had her stand up and I had my wife, Terrie Kay, stand behind as I led her in a forgiveness prayer. Then as we started praying for her I touched her forehead with one finger and she was slain in the Holy Spirit. I told my wife to lift her up. She got back on her feet and I touched her forehead again and again she went down. I said, lift her up again for the third time. This time when I touched her forehead, with my finger, she went down and her body started shaking like convulsions and she was screaming and praising God. She said, "I am healed. I am on fire."

When she went down this third time, a man came around the corner and said, "Oh you just knocked this woman down. I'm calling the cops." Then the Holy Spirit told me to say, "Mind your own business, I know my business." This time she didn't need help getting up. She just leaped up on her own and the Glory of God was sitting on her. The peace, the comfort, and the healing was so exciting. She sat down and was shaking her leg and was full of excitement. What a glorious day it was.

I often wonder what would have happened if I wasn't obedient. Would God have sent somebody else? I often laugh when I read her posts on social media, when she says she's fat. I laugh and say, "Lord, you remember when she was only 60 lbs?" Thank you God for this great healing of this wonderful remarkable lady.

THE FOLLOWING IS MARGE'S PERSONAL TESTIMONY.

"Marjorie Woods has had an amazing healing from an amazing God. In October 2018 I was diagnosed with colon cancer. The whole colon was taken out and I had an ostomy bag. I could only handle six of the twelve chemo treatments I had scheduled. From being in the hospital or ER after every treatment. It was physically and emotionally wearing me down to nothing. I decided I wasn't doing any more treatments. I was tired and done fighting. I knew the next step was telling my family, saying goodbye, and waiting for hospice to come in. But who knows God always has a plan.

In June of 2019, a childhood friend of my sons, named Billy Davison was giving the gift of healing from God. He contacted me and said he had a word from God and wanted to know if he could come pray for me. Billy and his wife Terrie Kay came to my home. Billy told me something was preventing me from being healed. He pointed out Mark 11:24-26 (NKJV) where it says God not cannot forgive us if we cannot forgive others. I immediately knew what he meant. I did have unforgiveness. It was toward my deceased daughter. Billy said if you want to be healed all you have to do is say Lord I forgive her. I boldly prayed to the Lord I forgive her.

Billy and his wife had me stand up and pray. He touched my forehead with his finger and I was slayed in the spirit. Each time I got up the Holy Spirit hit me again. The third time however a fire was going through my body and I knew I was being healed by the mighty hand of God! Since that glorious day I have felt the best. I went back to the doctor and they didn't recognize me. My hair has grown back and I'm at 130 lb. I am active. I walk daily and I get to play with my great granddaughter. We serve an awesome God."

SECOND TESTIMONY OF MARGE

"Close to a year after I was healed of cancer I started having trouble with my vision and gout on my foot. I again called Billy and told him I needed prayer. This time he brought his lovely wife, Terrie, and their daughter, Taylor, to pray over me and of course again I was slayed in the spirit. Since that day I have had no problem with my vision or gout in my foot. I profess I am healed. We have an amazing guy that heals, you have to fully believe in your faith. I am ready for what God has in store for me!!!" God bless Marge Woods

If God has an open, willing, and obedient vessel awesome healings and miracles can happen constantly. His love for us is unmeasurable and these testimonies build faith for the unbelievers and for the believers that their Faith isn't very strong. After close to a week and not being able to sleep, praying and meditating with the Lord I finally fell asleep. I was three minutes in rest and the Holy Spirit woke me up and said, "GET UP AND WRITE THIS!" The sermon that follows was 100% inspired by the Holy Spirit. Each line I wrote was tear stained.

"We need to "STOP" fighting with other denominations, about what they believe in and what they don't! We need to focus on Christ.

The only fighting we need to do is against the devil! Ephesians 6:12 (NKJV) says: "For we do not wrestle against flesh and blood, but against principalities, against powers, against the rulers of the darkness of this age, against spiritual hosts of wickedness in the heavenly places."

It's time we get into the scriptures and learn what we must do to prepare for battle. The book of Ephesians 6:10-18 (NKJV) says: "Finally, my brethren, be strong in the Lord and in the power of His might. Put on the whole armor of God, that you may be able to stand against the wiles of the devil. For we do not wrestle against flesh and blood, but against principalities, against powers, against the rulers of the darkness of this age, against spiritual hosts of wickedness in the heavenly places. Therefore take up the whole armor of God, that you may be able to withstand in the evil day, and having done all, to stand. Stand therefore, having girded your waist with truth, having put on the breastplate of righteousness, and having shod your feet with the preparation of the gospel of peace; above all, taking the shield of faith with which you will be able to quench all the fiery darts of the wicked one. And take the helmet of salvation, and the sword of the Spirit, which is the word of God; praying always with all prayer and supplication in the Spirit, being watchful to this end with all perseverance and supplication for all the saints—"

Yes, I'm a word of faith, tongue-talking Pentecostal, but I don't need a label, for I'm a Christian!!! The devil is the author of lies and confusion. 1 Corinthians 14:33 (NKJV) - "For God is not the author of confusion but of peace, as in all the churches of the saints." The scripture says the devil roams around the world like a roaring lion seeing who he can devour. 1 Peter 5:8 (NKJV) - "Be sober, be vigilant; because your adversary the devil walks about like a roaring lion, seeking whom he may devour." So many people are taught so many different things about speaking in tongues. Some say it's for today, some don't. All I can say is read the book of Acts 1:8, 2:4 (NKJV); Mark 16:17(NKJV); and Ephesians 6:18 (NKJV) which say "praying always with all prayer and supplication in the "Spirit."

If it wasn't meant for today it wouldn't be in the Bible. There are many, many, many, more examples. I'm just showing you how the devil goes and twists things and causes confusion. We know who that's from, NOT GOD!!!

(1 Corinthians 14:33 NKJV) "For God is not the author of confusion but of peace, as in all the churches of the saints." Rebuke that lying devil!!! "Then Jesus said to him, "Away with you, Satan! For it is written, 'You shall worship the Lord your God, and Him only you shall serve.'" (Matt 4:10 NKJV) The devil is not for us he is against us. The devil thrives on confusion and lies and destroys churches with whisper campaigns and idle gossip and lies, until they are weak and empty and that's when they start closing.

In The Gospel of John 8, Jesus tells us that Satan was a murderer from the beginning, and does not stand in the truth because there is no truth in him. Whenever he speaks a lie he speaks from his own nature, for he is a liar and the father of lies. When the power is gone out of church, the devil thinks he's won. But doesn't the scripture say in Matthew 18:20 (NKJV) "For where two or three are gathered together in My name, I am there in the midst of them." The requirement is to meet in his name, doing such by even two or three in the eyes of God constitutes a church. Everything I'm saying I am backing up with scripture to show you that the devil is a liar and a thief and he must be stopped!!! Christians fighting with other Christians. this not what Christ wanted, it is not what Christ wants now. So many churches are fighting with each other instead of fighting the fight against the devil and Sin. Those that know me, know I'm a healing evangelist, I pray in tongues. I'm not of the devil as some religions teach. I have many, many, many, written out testimonies from other believers, that have seen or know the great miracles and healings God our Father has done through me.

I don't care if you're Catholic, Baptist, Nazarene, Methodist, Presbyterian, non denominational, full Gospel, or charismatic. You want to see the Holy Spirit move, you want to see people healed, you need to move the devil out!! Jesus Christ himself said the two greatest commandments are to love God and love thy neighbor as thyself. (Matthew 22:37-38; Mark 12:30-31; Luke 10:27) Neither one of those commandments says we are to judge. You want to judge someone, judge yourself. Matthew 7:1-2 (NKJV) says, ""Judge not, that you be not judged. For with what judgment you judge, you will be judged; and with the measure you use, it will be measured back to you." 1 Corinthians 11:31 (NKJV) "For if we would judge ourselves, we would not be judged."; Luke 6:39 (NKJV) "And He spoke a parable to them: "Can the blind lead the blind? Will they not both fall into the ditch?".

Romans 3:23 (NKJV) "for all have sinned and fall short of God". Jesus Christ loves us so much he died on that cross so we wouldn't have to. Romans 6:23 "For the wages of sin is death, but the gift of God is eternal life in Christ Jesus our Lord." If you're a heathen living in sin it's not our job to put a spotlight on your sins or beat you over the head with the Bible. It's not for me to judge you, because I am unworthy also, of that great responsibility. Our jobs as Christians are to invite, encourage, and welcome you in with open arms and love into the house of the Lord. How can anyone feel welcome when they're being judged, and whispered about and glared at before they even can sit down. The church is a hospital for the sick not the saints. Mark 2:16-17 (NKJV), "And when the scribes and Pharisees saw Him eating with the tax collectors and sinners, they said to His disciples, "How is it that He eats and drinks with tax collectors and sinners?" When Jesus heard it, He said to them, "Those who are well have no need of a physician, but those who are sick. I did not come to call the righteous, but sinners, to repentance."

How can anyone feel welcomed when they're being looked down at. That's why bars are full of lost people because they're welcomed into those establishments. Isn't that just a little backwards. So many people are hurting and lost and wanting help. I can understand why they wouldn't want to go to church and be judged by all those perfect Saints, before you even get out of the car. John 3:17 (NKJV) "For God did not send His Son into the world to condemn the world, but that the world through Him might be saved." Well those perfect Saints are just lonely Ain'ts that want to point out the speck in your eye. Matthew 7:3 (NKJV), "And why do you look at the speck in your brother's eye, but do not consider the plank in your own eye?" Luke 6:41-42 (NKJV), "And why do you look at the speck in your brother's eye, but do not perceive the plank in your own eye? Or how can you say to your brother, 'Brother, let me remove the speck that is in your eye,' when you yourself do not see the plank that is in your own eye? Hypocrite! First remove the plank from your own eye, and then you will see clearly to remove the speck that is in your brother's eye." In John 8:44 (NKJV) Jesus is telling the perfect, religious people, the hypocrites - "you are of your father, the devil, and you want to do the desires of your father." Revelations 3:15-17 (NKJV) "I know your works, that you are neither cold nor hot. I could wish you were cold or hot. So then, because you are lukewarm, and neither cold nor hot, I will vomit you out of My mouth. Because you say, 'I am rich, have become wealthy, and have need of nothing'—and do not know that you are wretched, miserable, poor, blind, and naked—"

Brothers and sisters I love you. I have ended many days fast, I haven't slept in over 30 hours and after receiving a few hours of rest tonight, the Holy Spirit woke me from slumber and gave me this whole message to share. You want to see people healed? You want to see people saved (sozo)? You want to see people delivered? Well then you need to evict the devil and begin to walk in faith. Faith is an act, it is trust. Faith is not a life you live, it's an act you perform. In Hebrews 11:1 (NKJV) "Now faith is the substance of things hoped for, the evidence of things not seen.". Hebrews 11:6 (NKJV) "But without faith it is impossible to please Him, for he who comes to God must believe that He is, and that He is a rewarder of those who diligently seek Him." Hebrews 11:1-39 is a faith chapter. As soon as you step out on faith I guarantee the Holy Spirit will be there to guide your way. Hebrews 12:2 (NKJV) talks about looking unto Jesus the author and finisher of our faith.

Evicting the Devil and Blessing Homes

As born-again Christians we are all apostles of the Lord. And we have the power to do all these things in the name of Jesus Christ.

"And these signs will follow those who believe: In My name they will cast out demons; they will speak with new tongues; they will take up serpents; and if they drink anything deadly, it will by no means hurt them; they will lay hands on the sick, and they will recover." Mark 16:17-18 (NKJV)

"And through the hands of the apostles many signs and wonders were done among the people. And they were all with one accord in Solomon's Porch." Acts 5:12 (NKJV)

"Is anyone among you sick? Let him call for the elders of the church, and let them pray over him, anointing him with oil in the name of the Lord." James 5:14 (NKJV)

"Then the seventy returned with joy, saying, "Lord, even the demons are subject to us in Your name." Luke 10:17 (NKJV)

"Therefore submit to God. Resist the devil and he will flee from you." James 4:7 (NKJV)

From time to time people ask me to pray over their house, because weird things are happening. "I strongly advise that if you do not have the Holy Spirit living inside of you do not do this". In the 19th chapter of the book of Acts (NIV) verses 11-20 talks about this! "Do not go and do this if you're unarmed and unprepared."

THE SONS OF SCEVA

11 "God did extraordinary miracles through Paul, 12 so that even handkerchiefs and aprons that had touched him were taken to the sick, and their illnesses were cured and the evil spirits left them.

13 Some Jews who went around driving out evil spirits tried to invoke the name of the Lord Jesus over those who were demon-possessed. They would say, "In the name of the Jesus whom Paul preaches, I command you to come out." 14 Seven sons of Sceva, a Jewish chief priest, were doing this. 15 One day the evil spirit answered them, "Jesus I know, and Paul I know about, but who are you?" 16 Then the man who had the evil spirit jumped on them and overpowered them all. He gave them such a beating that they ran out of the house naked and bleeding.

17 When this became known to the Jews and Greeks living in Ephesus, they were all seized with fear, and the name of the Lord Jesus was held in high honor. 18 Many of those who believed now came and openly confessed what they had done. 19 A number who had practiced sorcery brought their scrolls together and burned them publicly. When they calculated the value of the scrolls, the total came to fifty thousand drachmas. 20 In this way the word of the Lord spread widely and grew in power."

Following are some wonderful testimonies of how the Lord has delivered some, healed some, and saved others.

That's Not Grandma

My wife and I got a phone call to come to someone's house. They said they had a ghost, she said when they saw it manifest it was an old lady, So they just assumed it was someone's grandma. She was shocked when she found out that demons manifest into anything. We went into the home with a mother and her three-year-old child. The mother called several weeks prior and asked for me to come and bless her house. Said the young child would not play in his room because he was scared of the old lady. They both would notice some things would move around the house occasionally, along with noises being heard. We showed up and I told her about Jesus and how in His name we have the power and authority to cast out demons. (Mark 16:17) As I walked through blessing the house, I kept preaching the Good News about Jesus Christ. And she gave her heart to the Lord, step one completed. Now let's do the next step and bless your house. As I walked through her house praying and rubbing oil on the doors and walls; I walked into the child's room and immediately it felt like a freezer and something tugged on the right back corner of my shirt. With the homeowner and my wife behind me witnessing what just happened, I started praying and evicting that demon from the house and commanding it to flee back to the pits of hell and never to return.

I felt the room warming up and a peace coming over it. I then started into another room and a clothes hanger got thrown at me.

My wife and the homeowner we're getting ready to make a new door and I just laughed and prayed as I continued casting out spirits from the house. As I finished, we walked into the living room and I laid hands on the young lady and immediately she was slain in the spirit and fell to the ground. She laid there and wept. We helped her up and as soon as she was back on her feet the Holy Spirit knocked her down again. We let her lay there for a few moments and just let the glory of the Lord come upon her. She got back up and said, "I've seen this on tv and just laughed, oh how fake that is." Then she said, "You touched me with one finger. I know it's not fake now."

The young lady, her son, and her mother all go to church now and have been saved just by seeing for themselves how the love of Christ has set them free. Praise the Lord.

The Poor Child

A long time family friend contacted me and asked if I could come talk to him and his family about the Lord. He had recently gotten custody of his seven year old granddaughter. She had been physically and emotionally abused in every way possible, before he got custody of her. They had been having trouble with her at home and in school. She was rebellious, always talking to herself, and talking back in several sinister voices. She would scream at the top of her lungs because someone was touching her and she'd be in a room by herself. My wife and I went to their home to tell them about Jesus and cast those demons off of that child. As soon as I walked in the door that little girl screamed in a manly voice "go away". A little rattled I continued, because in 1 John 4:4 (KJV) it says he who lives in me is stronger than he who lives in the world. I immediately asked them if they were saved? We believe in God, they said. I said, "Well the demons in hell believe in God and tremble". The scripture says in James 2:19 (KJV) that just believing there is a God isn't enough. You need a personal relationship with Jesus Christ. In the scripture John 14:6 (KJV), it says the only way to get to the father is through the son.

The family all chose to say the sinner's prayer reluctantly, but I believe in my heart they were sincere. They all got saved that night. As soon as I saw the young girl I could see something manifesting in her. I could feel the hatredness and stuffiness of the room. There were some sort of demons upon her. With what the poor child had been through and the look in her eyes I just started to weep. Her eyes were dark and you could tell something had taken over her body. I explained to the grandparents what I was going to do. I wanted to spend time praying over the little girl and anointing her and the house with oil.

My wife and I went from room to room blessing each room as we got to it. The power and Glory of the Holy Spirit was so strong that my wife was slain in the Spirit several times, while we were there. As I continued to pray over the child, after a couple hours of screaming, kicking, yelling, and her trying to bite me; I felt that whatever had a hold of that little child was weakening. She was finally staying still and not running through the house. She sat on her grandparents lap and I got on my knees and anointed her head one last time and she screamed it burned. Then all of sudden I felt the compassion of Christ upon me as I touched her little face. I rebuked the last and final demon, and I watched it leave her and darkness came off of her eyes. Now her eyes were shining the prettiest blue. Both her and I cried as a peace came across the whole house; I knew in my spirit the demons had left.

We prayed with the family and child again before we left. I explained to the family how important it is to get into a church and read the bible, and get filled with the Holy Spirit. Think of this metaphor, when a demon gets cast out of a body it's like a hollow Easter Bunny there's nothing there but space, and that space needs filled. If you don't get the Spirit of God in there, those demons will come back and they will be seven times worse. When we left the girl was doing wonderfully. Praise the Lord for his love and grace.

The Young Couple

A young girl contacted my wife and asked if we could come bless her house. She had just moved into a home with her boyfriend and said she kept hearing noises. Her boyfriend has two small children that are there occasionally. She wasn't sure what was going on in the home, but it frightened her because she's there most of the time by herself. She said that the children's toys come on and off without anyone in the room.

We went and talked to her and asked if she knew who Jesus was. She told us that she knew who Jesus was and that she did believe. After speaking with her and explaining about living in sin, she repeated and we started blessing the house. We went room to room with her, blessing each room. When we were done, we prayed over her. She started moving her leg and laughing. We asked her what was going on and she said my hip had a pinched nerve and she hadn't been able to move it much without pain in a while. After we prayed for you she said that all of a sudden she felt a heat and now she can feel it and move it around. Praise the Lord.

We then prayed over her for blessings and guidance from God, and as soon as I laid my hands on her she was slain in the spirit, and she was filled with the Spirit so much that she was laughing uncontrollably. Not too long after we left her house, her mother called my wife and asked what went on. Her mother said it was like she was on a high. She was sharing it with her mom, her boyfriend, her dad, and her siblings. She told her boyfriend that things had to change. She wanted to get married and get her life on track. She messaged my wife for an hour or two that night with questions about what to read in the bible. The following week her mom, her little sister came to our house to talk and she was saved. A couple nights after that, her little brother was at our house and asked me to pray for him, he is eight years old. Praise God. He works in the lives of all ages, and works in so many ways.

"He that believeth and is baptized shall be saved; but he that believeth not shall be damned." Mark 16:16 (KJV)

"For God so loved the world, that he gave his only begotten Son, that whosoever believeth in him should not perish, but have everlasting life." John 3:16 (KJV)

That verse is the greatest love story in the Bible, may God bless all who read these wonderful testimonies of the great and powerful works of the Lord Jesus Christ. God bless you sincerely.

"So then faith cometh by hearing, and hearing by the word of God." Romans 10:17 (KJV)

The Uninvited Guest

In May 2020, I was contacted on the phone about a possible haunting. I was asked by a young mother named Kelsey, if I could come to her house. She had some questions and some issues and asked if we could talk. She asked me about ghosts and if a house can be haunted. She Proceeded to Tell me about all the weird things that were happening. From hearing voices, to an uneasy feeling as being watched, to physically being pushed. She informed me that they were getting ready to move and were fearful of this entity and didn't want whatever it was to follow them to the new residence. I agreed to meet with her, but with moving and everything they put the whole situation on the back burner and didn't have me come. Hoping it would be out of sight out of mind. They moved into their charming little home about fifteen miles away from the prior activity, but something didn't seem right!

Right at the beginning things were happening there, as they were in the apartment complex that she just left. What made the young family get serious and call me, was one night while sleeping they were awoken by an eerie demonic audible voice saying "SHE'S ASLEEP". They felt something was getting ready to harm the family. The little child was also acting differently. She seemed to be crying a lot. They asked when I could come, as soon as possible would be nice. Please come over and help me! When I arrived at the home. The first thing I do before entering a home is pray for the family and tell them about Jesus. And let them know they MUST change their lifestyles. The Bible says in Matthew 12:45 that when demons get cast out of the body or a residence, that body becomes an empty vessel and if the Holy Spirit isn't immediately taking up residence in that body or home, than those demons will come back and they will bring other demons with them that are seven times worse!! Each time I do a home blessing I inform the families that they must immediately change their lifestyle. After I explain this and they understand I begin starting to bless the home.

As I entered the doorway there was a lot of grief and heaviness in the house. An uneasiness like something or someone was there. Immediately I was scratched, which happens every time I do this. Those demons know the Holy Spirit of God is inside of me and they want no part of it. They are alway scratching me or throwing things at me or across the house, they want me away from them. I grabbed my anointing oil and I began to pray over the family and the home and the Holy Spirit went to work, using me as an instrument to cast out the evil spirits in the house. I continued to pray and rub oil on every wall, window, and door frame as I walked through the home. I pointed out where the really bad spots were and they were amazed at how I knew that because it was 100% accurate and I said God told me.

Each room I anointed and prayed over you immediately could feel a peace come upon it. The young mother said it felt so peaceful and it hadn't felt that way since day one. As I finished with the main floor, she asked if I could do the basement and I said that is where the Lord was sending me. As we approached the basement door, Kelsey's mother was going down to find the light switch and I screamed at her and said stop, get away from it! As soon as Tonya backed away I started crying and praying in tongues. It was like time stood still, then all of a sudden the Holy Spirit said, "Go down alone". As I went down into the dark, wet, danki basement, I began shouting in tongues and praying louder and louder. After about fifteen minutes I asked the family to come down and join me. It's gone, they cried out excitedly.

The young family led me to the corner of the basement and said that is where they felt like something was going to leap out and grab them. Now it's peaceful. I said that's the first place the Holy Spirit led me. Was to that corner. After we returned upstairs Kelsey said that when storms would roll in, going to the basement was the last resort. Basements always seem creepy to me she replied, but mine felt like somebody was staring at me and was getting ready to reach out and grab me. I said don't worry kiddo it is gone now, it's up to you to keep it away. The only way is to bring Jesus Christ into the equation.

FOLLOWING IS KELSEY'S TESTIMONY.

"When it comes to demonic spirits and hauntings, I was never a believer; until I had something haunt my family and me. Upon receiving the joyous news that we were expecting a child my fiancé and I moved into a new apartment. Life was becoming more joyous as the days passed, or so I thought. Just weeks after moving in, I began to hear distant chatter throughout the day as I would sit home alone. The chatter would always sound like a small group of individuals talking in the room or hallway next to me. For a couple of weeks, I chalked it all up to my neighbors. Thinking it is quite possible that they have their tv up louder than usual. As the weeks went by, the voices started to progress. I would hear disembodied voices shouting my name all hours of the day and night, often waking me from a deep sleep. After being creeped out on several occasions and continuing to ignore it, it started to become more restless and hostile. I was about 28 weeks pregnant and heard the disembodied voices starting up at their usual time around 10 am. I decided I was not going to sit there and let them creep me out, so I grabbed my keys and headed down the stairs to leave. I got to the third step from the top and felt something push me back with extreme force, causing me to fall down the stairs. This continued every other day for about a year. Then it subsided for a while, and I would hear only disembodied voices for a couple of weeks.

Shortly after having my child in January of 2018, a shadow figure began to appear quite often. It would stand at the end of my bed or in the hallway most nights and often appeared on the video baby monitor in my daughter's room. After weeks of feeling stalked, the shadow began to start talking, always being heard clearly through the baby monitor. The shadow figure would move from room to room, following the baby everywhere she went. Soon after she turned one, it started to be drawn to her room more than ever.

One night the baby woke up crying so I checked the monitor and I could perfectly see a shadowy figure lifting her blankets off her and putting them back down over her while shushing her and saying "It'll be okay". After three nights in a row of it waking up the baby, we started to visibly see it walking up the stairs, into the baby's room and back down the stairs, while also hearing a baby cry every time it would make itself known or be on the move. I became extremely depressed and withdrawn, the baby seemed to be on edge all the time as well. As time went on like this we began to get sick. Sporadic nausea, and vomiting was a daily event as well as the feeling of oppression. Not knowing what to do, we moved. Just like when we moved into the apartment, things were calm and quiet for about three or four weeks.

One day out of nowhere, we began to see orbs of light. They would jet quickly around the house, through walls and end up in the bedroom with the baby. The baby soon quit sleeping due to nightmares. She would thrash around all night while screaming in her sleep the entire night. The same wave of depression began to wash over me as the maniacal spirit was back up to its old tricks. Same disembodied voices, same figures, same voice shouting my name, the same feelings of oppression, depression and being followed, but this time it was much more hostile. It started to move objects and personal items, open and close doors, and even emit smells of flatulence, smoke, or rotting flesh. After a long day of trying to ignore its attempts of getting my attention, the baby, my fiancé, and I all went to bed. After an hour and a half of the baby screaming, she finally fell asleep. As my fiancé and I started to drift off to sleep we heard a female's voice whisper, "She's out" as if she were in bed with the three of us. My fiancé and I shot up in a panic, as we were starting to feel helpless at this point. The next day we contacted my uncle, Billy Davison, curious about a house blessing. We set up an appointment for him to come and do the blessing on Friday May 1, 2020. That day was the day everything started to look up.

Billy came in and started the home blessing. Walking into the house that day, you could tell it did not want him here. The smell of sulfur filled the inside air. As we all prayed and Billy read scripture, you could hear it walking away from the group going into other rooms, up the stairs, and into the attic. When we reached the basement, the whole mood of the environment changed. We were all overcome by feelings of sorrow, grief, and anger. It was at this point that the baby and I were sent outside of the home to remain safe. Billy later came out and told us that we could come back inside so we did and all those densely negative feelings and overtones were gone. It felt like a clean home. We all said a prayer together before parting ways, and since that day, everything has been quiet, positive, and peaceful. All depression issues, night terrors, and disembodied voices stopped. There were no more orbs, shadow figures, or voices shouting my name; it is now peaceful, calm, comfortable, and quiet. I send my biggest thank you to Billy Davison for blessing my house; without his guidance and God's word I would be living just like I was in those apartment days, I will always be grateful for the help he has provided me with. Whatever was there is completely gone, our house is peaceful. What an awesome experience it was to see God move." Kelsey Marie

Seven is a Crowd

I n this ministry of the Lords, he has anointed me and I have seen a lot of miraculous things happen. God has used Terrie Kay, Taylor, and I in such phenomenal ways. Each time we are still amazed by the things He uses us for. From cancer patients being totally 100% healed, to seeing body parts develop right before our eyes. This exciting story I'm about to share with you is an interesting way of how the anointing power of God flows through me. Just touching someone's hand to pray, made a young lady start to manifest that was in bondage for decades from a demonic possession. And how she was delivered of something that has held her prisoner in her own body. Let me introduce you to Tammy. Following are testimonies about Tammy and her family.

"I just want to let you know a little bit about my background as we start. I was raised in church and I fell in love with Jesus when I was four years old. I can remember that like it was yesterday. I then grew up, and around age thirteen I started changing. I no longer really wanted to go to church, but I still had to twice a week. I then reached the age where I wasn't made to go to church anymore. I made a lot of bad choices, but I tell you this because I ran from God and my mother's prayers are what kept me safe. I'm not saying things didn't happen, because they did. The more I ran the more I hurt myself.

I got saved in June 1991 and received the Baptism of the Holy Spirit, and after I came out of the anointing I saw my dad with tears in his eyes. The second person I went to see was my Aunt Irene and my cousin, Billy Davison, who at this time was running from his calling. Just like I always have. Eventually I backslid. Here's my story:

I had been really struggling with the fact that I had skin cancer, I have worked in the medical field for years and I smelled cancer when my dad had it and I was cleaning. Anyway, I have always struggled with demonic activity. I had started babysitting for my first cousin's daughter in law, who is a "Witch", trust me. One day when she brought her son over, she knelt down to change her son and I could not break eye contact with her. I felt really strange, and my dog went after and almost had her by her face. My dog never does that. He surprised me. I barely got a hold of him and my sister, Kelli, came out and helped with him. My cousin's wife was very much taken off guard and I could tell she was angry. I don't remember the rest of the day, my sister said I was totally not myself after that.

Now that night I wasn't feeling well; I hadn't been feeling well ever since my cousin and her daughter in law started coming around. While I'm in the bathroom that night I smell cancer. I also knew that I felt something inside me, I knew it was a demonic spirit.

Out of the blue on May 27, 2020 at 10:52p.m., my cousin, Billy, texted me and said, "We need to get together soon and talk. Stay strong your needed. I love you." I definitely believe in divine appointment and know there's a time and place and the Holy Spirit will set it up. I love you very much cousin. I answered his text with, "Wow, that is weird, I was just thinking about you and God, weird I usually ignore messenger until morning. I'm kinda taken back a bit and said yes we do". Billy answered back, "Someone is trying to get your attention cousin, He loves you so much he gave you such a great calling. I really feel in my heart it's time to use it." I then said, "Thank you cousin, tears are falling. I've got to get back to God and I need you to lead me in the sinner's prayer in a church. Pastor

Carolyn has a church. I will contact her, I love you cousin. Stay strong your needed." I had just sat down on my bed and cried out to God and told him, "You have got to send someone Lord, I'm going to die." At that very moment is when my cousin, Billy, texts me. I had not seen him in years or even really talked to him. Now that is God.

Billy wouldn't stop, there is even more. Now he was on facebook and says he sees the numbers 62 and 63, thinking it was an address that God was sending him to. When I was at the cemetery that day with my Aunt Kay and Kelli looking at my mom and dad's tombstone, my dad had died at age 62 and my mom at age 63. My mom, Sheryl Maxine (Courtney) Hughes, was Billy's great aunt. She was sister's with Billy's grandma, Irene, whom she helped raise because when she was born my mom was 16 years old.

So anyways, Billy also explains that he was driving around and was led to a place that he thought was maybe an address that matches one of those numbers. Ended up the place that he was led to was my place. He had never been there before and had no idea where I lived. I had asked him on facebook what he saw while he was driving and it was confirmed that it was indeed my house. God is Powerful.

Now Billy comes over with his wife, Terrie, God bless her. What a team God has put in place here. Now the part that I can tell you. I pray for those of you that will go through this. Billy started praying and a scream came out of me, I couldn't stop. It was so loud, then followed by a voice that said, "She's mine, she is going to die!". My legs stretched so long, I couldn't do that and it hurt. I was spitting at Billy and trying to bite and hit him. One of these demons I know have had since I was young. I remember Billy telling it to look at him and the hate I can't even begin to tell you the hate I could feel.

My sister Kelli was there and I remember her sitting in a chair and then there was still more to come. Again, here we go casting out the last one, and that was the one I knew I had for years. Anyway, I could not control my face muscles or my body. Then I sat up and I could only whisper to Billy, trying to keep my eyes closed. I could tell this demon wanted to look at Kelli. I said get Kelli out of here and then I can hear Billy telling Terrie to hold my legs. I had seven demons cast out, and then Billy and Terrie went through the rest of the house an dcast others out. THANK YOU GOD IS ALL I CAN SAY. Thank you to my cousin for being obedient, and praise God he has given you Terrie, who behind every man God proves his most precious gift is your wife." Tammy Sue Hughes

"God, Billy, and Terrie strike again. Debra Ann (Hughes) Archdale was at my, Tammy's, house after our cousin tried to cause conflict with my sisters, Billy, and I. Well, lets just say Deb was pretty angry when Billy and Terrie showed up at my house. She tried to stay in the bathroom with her grandbabies, who were in the bathtub. Anyway Billy and Terrie talk and share for a while and slowly Deb's guard goes down and WOW. The Holy Spirit falls and Deb gets saved and she later tells Billy that she had no intention of getting saved and reunited with Christ. Deb had also backslid. This was just another way that our amazing God works." Debbie's testimony, in Tammy's words

"The night that Debbie reconnected with Lord got even better. Debbie's daughter, Cheyenne Elizabeth Archdale, and her grenson, Kadyn Joshua Teal Hale, gave their lives to Christ at eleven years old. Kadyn said, "I was afraid when I heard my grandma and I didn't understand what was going on." Cheyenne said, "I too was afraid, because of hearing my mother cry and I didn't understand what was going on."

Aunt Kelli was explaining to the kids, in the living room, as I came in and explained to the kids that this was their bloodline. Royal bloodline from their Grandma and Grandpa, Sheryl and Gary Hughes. Billy had said this to me and I had never thought of it that way. Kadyn and Chey had stood in front of Billy, holding hands and staying right together and said the sinners prayer. The Holy Spirit hit this house with a greatness I've not ever experienced. I'm crying as I write this even.

To see the Holy Spirit fall on these children and I could feel my mother and father. I know God was allowing them to see their granddaughter and great grandson give their lives to the Lord. There was such a power of anointing. Debbie's other grandkids loved it, they loved the prayer and they wanted to be a part of it. I was so overwhelmed, it was so amazing and showed how important we are to God.

This lasted for some time and Kadyn and Chey were so under the anointing that Kadyn looked at pictures and said, "I saw him.", pointing at my dad, his great grandpa, Gary Hughes, Sr. Chey said later that she felt Charity Ann Hale, Deb's daughter which had passed when she was three months old. That's God and his love. Only he can give this gift of loved ones being able to see their beloved ones being saved and rejoicing. I know Aunt irene was right there as well. My mom and Aunt Irene were always together. Aunt Irene was such a big part of our lives. Mom always said my kids are Sis's kids and her kids are mine. We were always together.

Kadyn and Chey of course want to start going to church wherever Billy is. They are doing good, Kadyn has a lot of questions about God. Chey has more understanding in the word of God. Kadyn told me he wants to be more like Jesus and heal people. All I can say is Billy and Terrie, God is going to use you in so many ways, and I'm so glad we share the same bloodline. Praise God. Thank you Jesus". In the words of Tammy.

In Need of Repair

"Hello my name is Kyler, I am the nephew of Billy Davison. I'd like to share my experience with you. As a teenager I have lived life wilder than most adults. I was unhappy and felt unloved. After I heard about the experience that my sister Kelsey had and that Uncle Billy delivered seven demons out of a cousin of ours. My cousin kept encouraging me to talk to Uncle Billy. So I decided to ask my Uncle if he could help me. I'm tired of being miserable, mad, and upset. He agreed to see me and we sat in his office for a few hours and I poured out why my soul to him. I told him about all the toxic things I've been doing and I asked him, "Do you think I have a demon in me?" He said, "What happens when I do this?" The Uncle Billy started speaking in tongues, and I just started feeling real jittery and twitching. He said yep you have a demon, so he took me into the other room where my Aunt Terrie Kay and Grandma were. Uncle Billy told Aunt Terrie and grandma that if he tells them to leave, then to get out.

All the sudden he started praying for me and he said, "God says if you give your life to Him that he will remove these demons". So on August 5, 2020 I gave my life to God. The next thing I know Uncle Billy touched my head and started praying for me. I started letting out a scream like somebody was stabbing a hog. I kept feeling like I wanted to lunge at Uncle Billy and rip my face off and pull the hair out of my head. Something was coming out of me, something I've never experienced before. Before I realized it, it was me and Uncle Billy sitting on the couch. I was crying and I felt this great piece. I never want to have that in me again. Contrary to what people think the devil is real, he's evil and he hates you and I. As Uncle Billy said he's here to steal, kill, and destroy. Thank you Uncle Billy. God bless you."

The Vision

"Hello, I would like to introduce myself. My name is Tanisha Jo. As being the oldest child of Terrie Kay and Billy I have heard stories of my grandparents and the way God used them. My daughter Amilia is the one that was resurrected back to life and the miracle that changed my dad and our whole family's lives forever. This is a story of what happened to me while on vacation and how thankful I am that my dad is obedient to what God says and shows him. Before we even left my car broke down, then my boyfriend's car broke down. Dad said he wanted Amelia to stay with him; he didn't want her to go on the 4th of July vacation. Dad was very busy with work and his Ministry. By the time he got home we had already left on our trip. I now see God was trying to get my attention, but I was stubborn and I was determined to go to Missouri.

So we arrived in Hannibal Missouri and we got checked into a motel and we started making our plans for what we were doing that evening. All of a sudden I got a message from my dad. The message said - Do not let Amelia out of your sight. That's all he said. Unbeknownst to me the Holy Spirit was telling him things that we're going to happen and he was relating them to my mom. Mom called and asked, "Where are the fireworks taking place?" I told her the people said the fireworks were by the water and there was a fair of some sort going on. Mom then said dad had a vision and that we shouldn't go to watch the fireworks. But if we decided to go to the fireworks anyway, then we needed to make sure that we kept hold of all the kids especially Amelia. Mom then proceeded to tell me that a guy was going to try and take Amelia. That the guy would take Amelia and then her lifeless body would be found in the water. We ended up playing in the pool at the motel before we went for supper. By the time we got done with supper and tried to find the fireworks; we missed them because we went the wrong way. We took so long the kids fell asleep before we got back to the motel. I knew this was God, there was no way my dad could know any of that. I am so thankful that he is obedient. God raised my child from the dead, so I know He has awesome plans for her and I also know that the devil is trying his hardest to do all he can to destroy her and all of us. Thank you Lord for keeping us safe."

The Rest Area

So not too long ago, maybe a few months. I was passing the Rail Splitter Rest Area on I- 55, and the Holy Spirit showed me an image and said that I would be praying for someone there. Fast forward to today, as I started out this am I said God show me how much you love me today. As I dropped my load in Elgin Illinois and I was heading back toward home; I needed to make a pit stop. I was coming up to the rest area and there was a closed sign. I thought I'll just go to the Dixie truck stop at the next exit. As I was coming past the rest area exit the Holy Spirit said pull in. So I pulled in, and went down and pulled into a spot, down by myself. I got out stretched, walked around my truck and waited. I said what's going on Lord?

The Holy Spirit said just wait. I climbed back in my truck and started sweeping out the driver's side and some guy said do you want an apple. I turned around and this older gentleman was offering me an apple. He said, "It's a Wisconsin Apple, they're really refreshing." Immediately I started remembering that snow white cartoon where the wicked witch offers Snow White an Apple, LoL. I think it was Snow White. I'm thinking, who offers someone an apple at a rest area, but I accepted it. He said they were heading back home to Memphis Tennessee and they felt like they should go into that rest area.

He said every time they've stopped during their trip they've talked to people about Jesus. And they asked me if I knew Jesus. I said, actually I am a minister. I have a healing ministry. He was very excited and he said he had a friend with him that had kidney failure. He asked if I would pray for him. I laid hands on the guy's lower back and he said his back was getting very hot. I said great you're getting healed. A few moments later he said his whole back was on fire, but the pain was completely gone. He said he didn't tell me, but he was having pains in his back also besides his kidneys. And the pain was completely gone. Well, praise God and give him all the glory. I told him this was a divine appointment for sure because a few months ago the Holy Spirit said I'd be praying for somebody here.

What makes the story more interesting is yesterday I had a trip to Elgin Illinois and there was another one today and I felt compelled to take it. So I knew God was doing something because I hate going to Northern Illinois. Isn't God awesome HE never skips a beat HE always has something great in store for us. Well, I just wanted to share this. I thought it was awesome. Have a great day. God bless you.

"If we had a true revelation of God's love we wouldn't spend a lifetime worrying about yesterday or stressed out and worry about tomorrow."

Billy Davison

Final Thoughts

In Matthew 6:34, Jesus tells us not worry about tomorrow. Worry is a cousin to fear. In 1 John 4:18 (KJV) it says, "There is no fear in love; but perfect love casteth out fear: because fear hath torment. He that feareth is not made perfect in love." A perfect love is called agape. The perfect love of God. The awesome thing is you don't have to work to get it. Some think you must do this or that in order for God to love you. And Brothers and Sisters that's just not true.

Okay parents picture this, I will love my children if they make the bed, clean their room, take out the trash, and do the dishes. That's not the case at all we would love them whether they helped out and did that or not wouldn't we? In the book of Luke 11:11-13 (KJV) Jesus asked, "If a son shall ask bread of any of you that is a father, will he give him a stone? or if he ask a fish, will he for a fish give him a serpent? Or if he shall ask an egg, will he offer him a scorpion? If ye then, being evil, know how to give good gifts unto your children: how much more shall your heavenly Father give the Holy Spirit to them that ask him?"

The gift of the Holy Spirit is given to those who ask. The love of God is only one of many free gifts that God gives us because He loves us. His love for us is why He sent the Holy Spirit to guide us and to teach us.

In the book of Lamentations 3:22, 23, it talks about this steadfast love that never ceases and his mercies never come to an end; they are new every morning. Over in Isaiah 49:16 (KJV) it says, "Behold, I have graven thee upon the palms of my hands; thy walls are continually before me.", wow that is love! Let's keep going, in Matthew 10:29,30 again Jesus himself tells us how much God loves us. He knows when the sparrow falls out of the sky to the ground. Are we not more important than that bird? Yes, He loves us so much He knows how many hairs are upon your head and when one drops down like a sparrow. God knows and He already has the remaining hair on your head recounted. Every minute of the day we are in His heart. In Luke 15:4 again He says He would leave the 99 to go find the one who went astray. All the different books all give us a glimpse of the perfect love, the pure and true love of God. And now these verses didn't say we have to do something to get His love, what an awesome father!

The most memorized scripture of God's love is John 3:16 (KJV) "For God so loved the world, that he gave his only begotten Son, that whosoever believeth in him should not perish, but have everlasting life." That one verse has so much to tell us. I believe we should look at what God is saying. For God so loved the world. From day one He wanted a relationship with us. In the book of Genesis it shows that God had a one-on-one relationship, He walked with Adam in the cool of the day. He gave his son. When Adam and Eve ate the apple that separated them from God and the only way to get that closeness back and the intimate relationship was to send His son to take away our sins that kept us from God! He does not want to be away from us. He doesn't want to just be our Father. He wants to be our friend, our companion. God loves us so much and all He wants is a relationship with you. He came to save us from an eternal death.

The word save is also known as "sozo" in the greek. What's the new testament written from? So what does sozo mean? I'm glad you asked. It means save, saved, healed, preserved, delivered; all the things that perfect love of God has done for us at the cross. Each and every testimony you're about to read will show the pure and true love of our Heavenly Father.

I want to start with my own testimony and story. First how a loving God came and left the 99 to come after me. I Believe you will be blessed and will be able to get a clear picture of the love of our Heavenly Father, how patient He is and He never gets angry when we fall and stumble. He loves us so much. I believe He cries when people are cast into the lake of fire. All He wants a close intimate relationship with each and every one of us, but many choose to be separated from Him. He said, "I will never leave you, I will never forsake you. I will be with you until the end of time." That's agape love.

The Splendors of life, the memories of the past, the excitement of the future. When I put God in my life it became extraordinary. As long as you're an open willing vessel the Holy Spirit can use you. If you surrender and be obedient HE'll take you places you never dreamed of. I hope by reading this you get a better understanding of how great God is and how much he loves YOU. In each of these testimonies they show the perfect unwavering love of God. Each personal story has the true thread of the Holy Spirit weaved into them. And connects each believer in the body of Christ. Each of these testimonies were told and written down to show the extraordinary love of God and to build and glorify the kingdom.

I pray you have been blessed by these testimonies and stories of the mighty powerful working hand of God. As Christians it's our job to edify and build up the name of the Lord. By spreading the good news of his word and His Marvelous ever working miracles. His love for us is a free gift as it's healing deliverance, prosperity, joy, and peace. Sinner or Saint we are all his children and we are all entitled to his gifts. Once we accept him as our Lord and savior, He comes to take your sins away. So let him, don't hold on to them no more.

Two of the greatest prayers you can ever pray is for help, and for God to show you how much He loves you today. God does love you and he will show you. It just takes a few minutes of silence, reminiscing, and remembering to look back at your life and seeing that God's Hand has always been upon you. People often say that it feels like God is a million miles away. God hasn't walked away from us, we've walked away from him.

When I preach I use this illustration that God is the true North and slowly if we're not living right we drift away. Picture the face of a compass as it points North. We are right there with him, but the temptations of life make us stumble and before we know it we are in the opposite direction of the Lord. The people that are lost and sent away from God and are thrown into the lake of fire, because they didn't want anything to do with God, not because God didn't want them. As we all know the Holy Spirit convicts us when we're not living right, so nobody has an excuse that God wasn't there. He was there. They chose to ignore Him and the punishment is to be away from God's love. Each and every one He judges, He loves. The ones that got tossed into Hell, He loves, but they didn't love him and it showed by their actions. I promise you that if you would get a true foundation and revelation of how much God loves you, it will rejuvenate and restore your life. You'll start loving people, even strangers, on a street. You will want to run up and just hug on them and love on them, because of the love of God that is inside of you.

As I was writing the finishing part of this book I was sitting in my office talking to the publisher about it. Then I caught myself daydreaming and gazing at the first of the painted walls of my office and the beautiful pictures that my daughter hung on the wall. I began reminiscing about my own past and the house. Then just how quick life goes by, a thousand years of our life here on Earth is one day to God. Our youngest child turned 18 this year. I'm four years from turning 50, four grandbabies here and one in Heaven. It seems like only yesterday I was sitting on my grandmother's lap listening to her read over and over to me the story of Jonah in the well. With not a care in the world, just a huge imagination and picturing this great fish and Jonah on the inside of the whale, with loss and despair crying out asking for forgiveness.

As we are approaching the holiday season, one of my favorite memories I claim is decorating our home for Christmas with my dad.

Ladders and lights and memories of simpler times. Then waking up from a winter slumber, with the flashing lights of a strobe light on my bedroom wall and a rumbling sound of a snow plow pushing off the freshly fallen snow. Remembering my aunt's homemade eggnog and how much I loved the beautiful site of the first snow. So many of my loved ones have gone home to be with the Lord and the older I get I really reminisce and cherish those memories so much. God was always a permanent fixture in our lives. We were raised in an Assembly of God Church. Every time the doors were unlocked we were there.

People don't realize we need a foundation, without God it's like building a house on the sand and the tide moves in and destroys it. In Matthew 7:24-27, it talks about a foolish man and the wrong foundation. Since Genesis 1:11-12, we have lived in a wonderful world where trees are green, skies of blue, multi colored flowers, raging rivers, peace and tranquility. We are so blessed and loved by all the beautiful things that surround us and many of us take them for granted. I encourage you to take your Bible and go sit somewhere quiet, away from the city traffic, honking and screaming and just meditate and listen for God's voice. He will talk to you. Jeremiah 33:3 (KJV) says, "Call unto me, and I will answer thee, and show thee great and mighty things, which thou knowest not."

Thank you so much for reading this. I pray it has blessed you abundantly and gave you a greater revelation of the pure agape love of God. Jesus Christ loves you and so do I. God bless you. Billy Davison

Quotes, Antidotes, Funnies, and Encouraging Words I Have Shared

- "Beloved, let us love one another, for love is of God; and everyone who loves is born of God and knows God. He who does not love does not know God, for God is love." (1 John 4:7, 8 KJV) To call someone "Beloved" has so much of an impact rather than simply calling someone loved. Synonyms for Beloved are precious, adored, darling, dear, dearest, precious, favorite, cherished, treasured, prized, esteemed, much loved. If people could get a full revelation of how much God loves them, it will totally transform the way you look at God. It isn't God loves you, yes thank you, God loves you too. It's WOW, God loves me. "But the very hairs of your head are all numbered."(Matthew 10:30 NKJV) "But the very hairs of your head are all numbered. Do not fear therefore; you are of more value than many sparrows." (Luke 12:7 NKJV) "Before I formed you in the womb I knew you; Before you were born I sanctified you; I ordained you a prophet to the nations."(Jeremiah 1:5 NKJV) "So God created man in His own image; in the image of God He created him; male and female He created them."

(Genesis 1:27 NKJV) God bless you brothers and sisters, stay encouraged Jesus loves you and so do I."

- "Jesus Christ was the greatest expression of love that ever came on the face of the Earth. Yet as far as it is recorded in the Bible, he never said the words "I love you". Isn't that amazing? The greatest expression of love never said, "I love you". Do you know why? It's because love is more than words. It is action; 95% of Love is nonverbal. It is not in the things you say, it's what you do. In 1 John 3:18 (NKJV), "My little children, let us not love in word or in tongue, but in deed and in truth." To love in the world is to speak loving words, but to stop short of doing anything to prove that love. Love is an action. John 3:16 (NKJV), "For God so loved the world that He gave His only begotten Son, that whoever believes in Him should not perish but have everlasting life." Don't say you love someone, show them! Very often, in my prayer's of the day, I often ask the Holy Spirit to show me how much HE loves me. I am never disappointed with the results. Have an awesome day my friends. Jesus loves you and so do I. God bless you sincerely today."

- "Well good morning, let us praise, worship, and thank God for another day on this beautiful Earth. The Holy Spirit keeps leading me back to post about love. When you can see the grace of God and how much HE loves us. WOW. I'm telling you brothers and sisters it will be life-changing. We need to update our ways of thinking and being taught, and really study what the word says. We need a spiritual upgrade. So many teach that God only loves us if we do this and he loves us less if we don't do that. That's just not so. Right now He loves us as much as He possibly can. Whether you're leading a church, or sitting on your couch eating popcorn, or melting your brain with garbage on TV. You can not work toward or escape the mighty love of God. He passionately loves you. It's not love from a distance; He is pleased with you, He likes you, He loves you. We really need to get away from the teachings that God is always mad and angry with us! That's just not the case. He isn't ready to hit us with a bolt of lightning. Yes, in the old testament you see and read about God's anger. But all the anger God had for the people on Earth was taken at the cross. God loves us so much that He sent his son to die for you, "For God so loved the world that He gave His only begotten Son, that whoever believes in Him should not perish but have everlasting life."(John 3:16 NKJV). Jesus went to hell and rose from the dead to forgive us of our sins. God had His son go all through that because God wanted that intimacy back that He had lost with us. When you can get a total revelation of the true love of God, it will begin to change your life. Blessings will start to flow abundantly. It will transform you from who you are to the updated version. When you see how much God loves you, you'll be walking in the fruits of the spirit more easily. You'll be able to love others so much greater. I'm telling you brothers and sisters it's transformed my life. I knew God loved me but, I never realized how vast that love is. How He has made that love a personal love, toward each one of us. We are his favorite, if he carried a wallet our pictures would be in it; that's how much HE loves us. And I promise if you get a revelation of it, it will change your life. I love my wife, but after I really understood His love. It has transformed our marriage of 26 years. You'll get to a place where you don't care if people talk bad of you or don't like you. You just love and pray for them more, and say that's okay because God loves me and that's all that matters! When people slander my name I just hope they spell it right LOL Well, I pray you have an awesome and very Blessed day. Jesus loves you and so do I."

- ""For I am persuaded that neither death nor life, nor angels nor principalities nor powers, nor things present nor things to come, nor height nor depth, nor any other created thing, shall be able to separate us from the love of God which is in Christ Jesus our Lord." Romans 8:38,39 (NKJV) Wow nothing can separate us from the love of God. How awesome is that? I encourage you today to just meditate on how much God loves you! God's love isn't based on what we do for Him; and unfortunately this is how the world displays his love. If you do this or do that or give or go, God will love you more. That's just not true! Right now, God loves you as much as HE possibly can or ever has or ever will! There's nothing you can do and there's nothing that can keep you from HIS true agape love! Have a blessed day. Jesus loves you."

- "God loves people infinitely more than you do. If you want to see someone saved, healed, or delivered; it's because God, Himself, has touched your heart and has given you a revelation of how much He loves you! If you desire that passion it's definitely not from our human nature. Man's nature is selfish and not to care for anyone, but ourselves. If you have compassion to see others touched it's because God is already working on you. He's the one that gives you that compassion. The true love of God that's in you is what makes you want to see other things change. So many people think and teach that God is angry. And that's just not true. Jesus did such an effective job taking our sins away! Now God has an opportunity to love us and have that one-on-one relationship like He planned from the beginning. We believe the devil's lies and ignorantly we embrace religions warped views. Instead of studying for ourselves how much God really loves us. I know I sound like a broken record at times, but if everyone would get a true revelation of God's love, this world would do a 360 degree turn. I truly believe you'll start seeing blessing's because you'll start understanding God's love. Well have a great day God bless you. Jesus loves you and so do I."

• ""But seek first the kingdom of God and His righteousness, and all these things shall be added to you." Matthew 6:33 (NKJV) Brothers and Sisters, if we focus on the kingdom of God and put His interest first; you will start seeing a lot of things manifest. Abundant blessings, healings and miracles. Many of us are not focusing on the kingdom! We're focusing on our mountain "aka" our problem. We are all guilty of this. For example, if the doctor gave you bad news or a bad report, in the flesh we would immediately focus on that report instead of the one who says, "who Himself bore our sins in His own body on the tree, that we, having died to sins, might live for righteousness—by whose stripes you were healed." 1 Peter 2:24 (NKJV) In this verse in Matthew 6:33 (NKJV) Jesus is giving you a promise. "But seek first the kingdom of God and His righteousness, and all these things shall be added to you." Jesus is saying don't focus on the pain, don't focus on the mountain of problems, focus on me (Jesus). I preach a lot about the love of God and this verse goes with that. If we focused on God as much as we focused on ourselves or our problems, our lives would be transformed. The blessings, miracles, and healings would hit your life like the numbers on a lottery ticket. You wouldn't be able to get away from all the blessings that God has for you. But they will never manifest if you don't seek him 100% with your heart. I have problems just like everyone else, but I put my focus on the kingdom and those problems fade away fast. If God put in the Bible that we can have anything we ask for in the name of Jesus; (John 14:13, Matthew 18:19, Matthew 21:22, Mark

11:24 - NKJV) then He meant it, but we've got to take the first step! I love you all very much. God bless you this wonderful morning love you."

- "I want to talk to you this morning about understanding God's love towards us. Many are trying to work hard to please God because they think that's what it takes to get God to love them and that's just not true. The scripture that we know is John 3:16, NKJV "For God so loved the world that He gave His only begotten Son, that whoever believes in Him should not perish but have everlasting life." God so loved the world. That means everyone whether you believe in him or not, God loves you. The word whosoever, that is you; You, I, and we are whosoever. Over in 1 John 4:7,8 (NKJV) it reads: "Beloved, let us love one another, for love is of God; and everyone who loves is born of God and knows God. He who does not love does not know God, for God is love." Again, God is love no matter what you do or haven't done, God is absolutely one hundred percent in love with you. He has nothing but good plans for you. I know I'm going to step on some toes here, but contrary to what we've been taught God is not mad at us. He's not angry! God isn't standing in heaven with a lightning bolt ready to hit us when we fall or stumble. It's so sad that religious teachings have covered up the true love of God; by teaching He's angry with us all the time. Again that is not true. He is not angry, he's not sitting there in heaven with his arms folded and a disappointed look on his face. He loves us and the book of Jeremiah 31:3 (NKJV) says, "The Lord has appeared of old to me, saying: "Yes, I have loved you with an everlasting love; Therefore with loving kindness I have drawn you." God is not concerned about our performance, and we cannot disqualify ourselves from the love of God. I know we feel unworthy of such a great pure love and we try to hide our sins from God, but he knows every thought and action we do, and he is still 100%, completely in love with us. How awesome is that? Refer to Psalms 39:1-24 (NKJV). When we fall he's not ashamed and he's not angry, he still loves us. When I was a little boy, I tried to learn how to ride a bicycle without training wheels. My dad knew I was going to fall. And when I did was he angry? No, he wasn't. He ran over and picked me up, brushed off the dirt and love on me, and then asked if I was okay. Well, brothers and sisters in life we are all that little boy and girl on a bicycle and God is our Heavenly father picking us up and brushing off the dirt and loving on us. I promise you if you get a revelation of just how much God loves you it's going to ruin you, in a good way. You won't be so concerned about how others feel about you. You will just smile and say that's okay because God loves me and that's all that matters. Well stay encouraged my friends and be blessed."

- "Most of us think we really understand the love of God, but our experiences prove otherwise. We feel lonely, depressed, discouraged, and defeated. Every one of these negative emotions will be turned into a positive by the proper revelation of God's love toward us. Every time I preach the love of God people immediately shut it off. They always say, "Yes, I know how much God loves me." If you know how much God loves you, then why are you depressed? Why are you discouraged? Why do you feel defeated? In the book of Psalms It says "Let them shout for joy and be glad, Who favor my righteous cause; And let them say continually, "Let the Lord be magnified, Who has pleasure in the prosperity of His servant". (Psalms 35:27 NKJV)

John 3:16 (NKJV) tells us what God did because He loves us so much. Sisters and Brothers I'm telling you if you get

BILLY DAVISON

a revelation of how much God loves you it will transform you. If you say a four letter word today make it love! Love and Hate are both choices, but ultimately it matters what you do with it. I encourage you to choose love. Take the stranger on the street or the person that just cut you off in traffic and look at them through God's eyes; immediately the anger will go away and you will find a little peace. Well have a happy Friday. God bless you! Always remember Jesus loves you and so do I."

• "There is no one in the world that loves you more than God! We all have some scars from being used, mistreated, abandoned and hurt by others. Some scars are deep, some are not, but each scar made teardrop's fall. Man's love is not perfect, but the agape love of God is complete perfection. The scripture says, "Before I formed you in the womb I knew you; Before you were born I sanctified you; ordained you a prophet to the nations." (Jeremiah 1:5 NKJV) "So God created man in His own image; in the image of God He created him; male and female He created them." (Genesis 1:27 NKJV) "But the very hairs of your head are all numbered. Do not fear therefore; you are of more value than many sparrows." (Luke 12:7 NKJV) God knows every aspect of our life. He said that He would never leave us or forsake us in Hebrews 13:5 NKJV. He also promised He'd be with us until the end of time in Matthew 28:20 NKJV. He then said that He collected every teardrop we ever lost in Psalms 56:8 NKJV. Some people are taught and believe that God loves us less, than our loved ones on Earth. And He's always angry with us or we got to do this or that to gain His love! We don't have to do anything for God to love us! If we're out winning souls for the kingdom, or sitting on a couch eating potato chips and watching how the stomach turns on tv, God loves you the same!

78

What does God hunger for? Intimacy with us, a one-on-one relationship. He doesn't just want to be our Heavenly Father, He wants to be our friend, and our companion, our love. So this is for the individual that thinks no one cares about them and are having suicidal thoughts. God loves you and He's reaching out to hold you in his arms caressing your hair and kissing your brow He loves you like a father, He loves you like a buddy. He is your friend. If this message is for you please don't hesitate to reach out to me! God is not angry with you. He loves you and He's reaching out for you. Jesus loves you so do I."

- "Well good morning brothers and sisters, may God bless you abundantly this day. In 1 Thessalonians 5:18 (NKJV), Paul wrote "in everything give thanks; for this is the will of God in Christ Jesus for you." Paul is saying directly no excuses no exceptions in everything give thanks. Thank you Lord for this wonderful day that you have made. Thank you God for this opportunity for my brothers and sisters to read these words. I believe in divine appointment and I believe if you're reading this right now, it is the exact time the Holy Spirit wanted you to pick it up. May you be blessed and encouraged by these testimonies I pray for the blood of the Lamb to cover you and your family and keep you protected from the devil's schemes as written in Ephesians 6:11(NKJV). Again I thank God for you and His pure agape love for all of us. Be blessed and encouraged."

- "If we all lived the way that our heavenly Father intends for us to live, what a wonderful world this would be. You know my friends, we are all going to die sometime right? Then why not follow someone who promises us a better life after death? It's either a wonderful life in heaven or suffering in hell; either way you choose it's for eternity, so why not choose GOD. I must say I've seen a lot of people complain about the summer heat if you hate this heat, I gotta say you won't like hell. You may want to think about it because we aren't promised tomorrow."

- Most people know I have a healing ministry, I lay hands on the sick and see God heal them. Sometime I need to share with you all the great testimonies people have sent me about their healings in my four years in the ministry. They are very awesome!! I wanted to share with you what has been going on this week. So Wednesday night I preached my first sermon, Thursday afternoon I preached my second one. And close to a year of going to Shepherd's gate Foursquare Church Terrie Kay Davison and I are becoming members today. We are really blessed. People don't realize God loves us so much. If he has a mantle over a fireplace our pictures would be on it. If he carried a wallet our pictures would be in it. We are blessed in so many ways that we take it for granted. There's nothing we can do to make God stop loving us! So many people tell me God's mad at me for my lifestyle. That's a lie from the pits of hell!!! God's not mad at you, He loves you. When people die and go to hell it's not because God doesn't love them; it's because they don't love God. If you're saying, Billy I have fallen short God can't forgive me, I have really messed up. That's not true. The scripture says we all have sinned and fallen short of the glory of God. It doesn't matter what you did. All that matters is if you are truly sorry, Repent and God will forgive you. He loves us so much he gave us free will. And that free will makes us live a life away from God sometimes. Please don't ever think God turns his back on us; we turn our back on Him. Jesus loves you and so do I. Be blessed today, stay encouraged, chin up. God bless. (Oct 26, 2019)"

- "I just used this story in class today, I think I will share it with you all. A while back someone sent me a message on facebook telling me they were unfriending me because I am taking this Jesus thing too serious! My response before I was blocked was, "Dearest friend 2016 years ago there was a man that was beat with a whip type tool 39 times on his bare back and chest, then spit on and someone took a crown of sharp thorns and forced them on his head. And if that wasn't enough they made him carry a heavy cross a few miles outside of town as more people cursed him. When he finally got to the hilltop they drove long nails into his hands and feet and then into the tree that he carried and they stood him up for all to see until he died. You know what my ex friend, I don't think I am serious enough about this man because he went through all of that because he loves you and I." Then I was blocked, but my friends, brothers and sisters; let me say I don't care what you think of me or say about me, I love you as does JESUS. And I pray daily for you all."

- "I was working on a sermon today and I was thinking about the world of sin. The devil makes things so appealing that we are drawn in. For an example look at a bar. On the outside there are all these very beautiful colors of lights, but as soon as you step in its dark. This is because the devil is the Prince of darkness. We have a bug zapper and almost each night I just sit out and watch it, and I've done it for years. I watch these bugs seeking to get closer to this beautiful blue light until they are so close it kills them. Ok, so where I am going with this, well while we live in the world we live in sin and like the bugs we get closer and closer to this deadly thing (sin) until ZAP your dead. It happens that fast and before you know it you're either in one place or another. I knew a lot of people in my wild life. I was one of them who said I'll change this or after I quit doing this I'll seek GOD, but the problem is many never get that chance because we are not promised tomorrow. I don't care what your sin is JESUS CHRIST can take it from you in his time. If you smoke, drink or whatever, Jesus doesn't care he wants a relationship with YOU. And then he will free you from whatever your battles are. I'm telling you this from experience I did a lot!!! I broke all but two commandments. I was the man who said when I stop doing this I'll look for God. Well I've seen too many friends die saying the same thing and I love you all so much I want to help you. Because I want to see you again someday in heaven. It's ok to message me and ask questions. Many aren't ashamed. Jesus said if you're ashamed of me before man I'll be ashamed of you before my father. Let's pray: "Heavenly father I thank you for this beautiful day and I thank you for all my wonderful friends on facebook. I pray you will walk with them today and meet them where they are in their life. Lord I thank you for the many blessings you have poured out on to my life and the ones that are coming. Lord please fix broken and hurtful hearts and father and daughter relationships. Lord walk with us today as we go unto the world. Give us the wisdom and knowledge to speak your word. I love you father and I am thankful you saved me before it was too late. I pray that this message goes to whomever you want it too. Have a great day everyone and stay safe. In the blessed name of Jesus I pray. Amen.""

• "Once there was a little bird who fell out of his nest. He got really cold sitting there on the ground so he started to peep, "PEEP, PEEP, PEEP!" A cow heard his cries and came over. Seeing the shivering bird the cow turn around and plopped a huge cow patty on top of the little bird. Now the little bird was warm and that made him happy, but he started to peep again, very loudly "PEEP, PEEP, PEEP!" A coyote was passing by and heard the loud crying bird. He came over and with his paw, scooped the birdie out, cleaned all the dirt off him and popped him in his mouth! GULP! The moral? Not everyone who throws dirt on you is your enemy and not everyone who pulls you out of it is your friend. So when your neck deep in poo, it's best to keep your mouth shut."

- "I'm so tired of people saying do crunches do crunches you'll lose weight!!! I'm on my second case of Nestle crunches. The only thing I have lost is the sight of my feet."

- "How do you prepare to say the last goodbye to someone who had such a great impression on your life? I prepare to touch your still hand while knowing the teardrops will start to fall. As the memories of you start to flow like a river. And an echo of your laughter ringing in my ears. I can't help but imagine the awesome reception that's going on in heaven. I know death isn't the end, but a wonderful and glorious beginning. I know I will see you again, but when? So many have gone home, and I can't help but feel alone. I'm glad you're at rest and you're not suffering anymore. And I know these teardrops will pass. And my memories of you will forever last. I just want to thank you for the memories. God has truly blessed me when he made you a structure in my life. Your advice about love and life is displayed today in my family. Your knowledge of many things was abundant, and you always took time to share your wisdom. Thank you for everything. Rest in peace."

- "I pray God, will bless you, and let you live as long as you want! And you'll never want as long as you live. And the last voice you will ever hear will be mine. God bless you."

- "Thank God I don't have to hunt for food I don't even know where Twinkies live."

- "If you want to know if an elderly person is on medical marijuana, just count how many times meals on wheels stop at their house. LoL"

- "Well I'm finally at that point in my life, where the only thing that is thin is my hair!"

- "I am so depressed I have been on a diet for two months and I couldn't figure out why I kept gaining weight. Dang you Extra Body Shampoo. LoL"

- "You can tell alot about a woman by the position of her hands. If they're around your neck she's probably slightly upset!"

- "As I grow older, I see more and more loved ones called home. And from time to time, I take more and more opportunities to reflect on their absences from my life. The memories and laughs that we shared. I will always hold those precious memories in my heart until I'm carried to the grave. The scripture says a thousand years to God is like one day, they are like yesterday already gone. As I reminisce of my final earthly days. A great many are behind me now, as I draw closer to the 50-year mark. With perhaps only a few more days ahead of me. Looking back I can say I have been blessed. And looking forward to the future I have joy and sorrow. Sorrow that my race is almost run and it will be over at any time. But joy knowing that I'll be welcomed home with my loved ones for eternity. Don't weep for me, this world isn't my home. But Weep for the lost that don't know God and his very precious Son Jesus Christ. For you can only get to the father through the son. May God bless you and your family this evening."

- "The three greatest things you can give someone in my opinion are.

1) Lead someone to Jesus Christ
2) A Bible
3) Your time

God loves you so much that he sent his son to redeem you and I of our sins. God bless you."

- I wrote this last night for my Uncle Leroy it's called My uncle ...

My uncle
The time has come to say goodbye. It's hard to breathe and I just sit and cry. You are more than an uncle to me, you played the part of my grandpa, for mine I didn't really know. Then you became like a father when mine passed away a few years ago. We spent many days just chewing the fat and talking about the yesterday's that disappeared just like that. I tried to soak up all the wisdom and knowledge you had stored, and see life through your aging eyes. A man that I just adored. I still own some of your favorite trains, but I would sell them all today to hear you laugh again! You were such a great person, you were such a wonderful friend, our talks and the visits I'll surely miss. I thank God daily for your special kindness and for the times I shared with you. Your memory will remain deep in my heart. It's a little shattered and broken and falling apart, but you being ill is also tearing me apart. I know you're in the hands of God and that's the best place to be. Our life on Earth is just

temporary. Jesus has somewhere else better for us to be. I know someday I'll talk and laugh with you again until that time goodbye my Uncle, my Pal, my Friend.

- "Does anyone else have the problem when giving your cat a bath, getting their hair stuck to your tongue??? Asking for a friend. LoL"

- "As I remember as a kid my parents said to be home when the street lights came on, thinking back our town didn't have street lights."

- "When I was a kid my family moved a lot. As I get older and I reminisce of my childhood the only thing I regret about it is now I wish they had taken me with them."

- "You'll never be able to live in peace if you can't be open and honest about your downfalls due to your sinful past. After I rediscovered Christ and repented, freedom has entered my life. Never again would I have to hide skeletons in my closet. I ripped off the door and exposed them. You'll never be able to move forward if you're always hiding something from the past. Thanks to the grace and mercy of Jesus Christ, I can move on and be free. He truly has set me free of the shackles of the past. I encourage everybody to rip that Band-Aid off. Yes, at first there's a lot of hurtful feelings and tears, but the peace it brings to you is worth it trust me, I promise. God bless you."

- "Without Christ I am nothing!!!! But with Him I can destroy Hell for a living!"

- "The Holy Spirit hasn't sent me to point out your flaws, he sent me to show you the Mercy, Grace, and Unconditional Love of Jesus Christ."

- "Oh how I miss the days of dating. I remember how great it was that if I would cancel a date with a girl it would take two cops and a preacher to keep her from jumping."

- "Love one another, it is not a recommendation, it is not an option; it is a COMMANDMENT!"

- "I quit subscribing to newspapers, because the stories kept changing."

- "When we look at the bright sun; how the rays shine down on us, then all sudden the clouds come and cover the sun. Now we all know that the sun is still shining. It's just covered up. What needs to happen to get the brightness of the sun back? Yes, we have to remove the clouds. The same thing applies with God. The love of God toward us is constant; it never changes. Sometimes problems get in our way and block us from seeing the Lord, but He's still there. What we need to do is hand those problems to him. So he can take away that interference. I know at times you feel all alone, but you never are. We just allow problems to block us from our father. No matter what you do or think or say or stumble or fall; He still loves you immensely. So don't let the devil lie to you and tell you because you stumbled, God doesn't love you. That's a lie. Nothing can keep you from the love of God. Have a great weekend. Jesus loves you and so do I."

- "You know as I was sitting in my office yesterday talking to a publisher about my book. I was looking at my freshly painted walls and the beautiful paintings my daughter hung.

I began reminiscing about my past. I am just stunned how fast time goes by. Our baby turned 18 and he's a senior this year. I'm 4 years from 50. I have four grandbabies here and one in heaven. It seems like only yesterday I was sitting on my grandma's knee listening to her read the Bible, with not a care in the world. As We are approaching the holiday season; one of my favorite memories I cling to is decorating our house for Christmas with my dad. Ladders and lights and memories of a simpler time. Being woken up from a winter slumber while the flashing light and the rumbling sound of a snow plow pushing the snow off the roads. To Aunt Linda's homemade eggnog. And The beautiful sight of the first snow. So many of my loved ones have gone home. I guess that's why I talk and reminisce and cherish these memories so much. Life, it was just a simpler time then. I don't ever remember locking our doors. Even at night when we slept we left our doors unlocked and open all night in the summertime. If there was such a thing as an atheist we never heard of them. We all loved God. And were proud of our country. Childhood Sundays were the best. You see friends and neighbors rushing around to get ready for church then all of a sudden the town was like abandoned. Doors unlocked. Homes were vacant and Churches were full. After church was a big family dinner with grandparents. aunts, uncles, and cousins. Every week that was our routine. As a few of us still try to keep that old time value of family get-togethers sacred and continue a tradition of long ago. But it is met with opposition, and excuses why they don't have time. I am very guilty of this myself. Sadly after loved ones go home our great strong foundations start to crumble and break away, and we fade our way out from others. Family's start to break up and no new memories are made. I encourage everyone this holiday season to make an effort and just stop in to say hello. With our busy schedules we don't realize how much it will bless others just to stop and say hi. Well, I pray you all have an awesome day. And if I don't see you again I know I'll walk with you again in heaven. God bless you Jesus loves you and so do I."

- "I'm a Christian, but not quiet. I don't want to make waves kind of Christian. I'm the Jesus flippin tables kind!!!"

- "We must stand and let the world Know Jesus is the light and we won't hide Him under a basket. It's out of love I want to tell you about Jesus. Don't let the lies of the devil keep you from the perfect love of God. It doesn't matter what you have done, you can be forgiven and walk out of shame and into love. Look at King David, he had an affair with his soldier's wife, got her pregnant and then murdered the soldier. And the bible says David was a man after God's own Heart. If God can forgive David of his sins, He will forgive yours also. You don't have to be a prisoner to your sins any longer. Stay encouraged Jesus loves you and so do I."

- "Jesus doesn't have covid-19 so you don't need to stay six feet away from Him!!!!!!"

- "Does your family suffer from mental illness? No, they all seemed to pretty well enjoy it. Lol"

- "So many love and care for you, but your drama is slowly pushing them away, and at the end of your time, you'll be alone and miserable because nobody wanted to be around the poisonous negativity that you spewed out. Can't you see it's already happening, the ones that truly love you and matter are not around anymore. They loved you so much and always tried to help you, and show you what true unconditional love is. But you keep relying on your so-called friends that are wolves in sheep's clothing. I Don't mean to sound blunt, or hateful and I don't want to hurt you at all because I love you also! We know you have a great heart, you're just so mixed up because so many people replaced lust with love and that cut you deeply. As much as they hurt you, you have to let go and move on. Please see what you're doing to everybody that cares and matters for you, there slowly going away. There's still time to change and bring them back before it's too late. I love you, I'm a phone call away to help!!! Please see that. God bless you kiddo."

- "Isaiah 49:16 NKJV. "See, I have inscribed you on the palms of My hands; Your walls are continually before Me." (WOW) If people would get a true revelation and understand how much God loves us, I believe it will be a game changer in so many lives. So many people think if I do this for the church or if I do this or I do that God will love me more, that's not true! Yes, those things bring the Lord Joy. but that doesn't make him love you any more or less. We've got to adjust our thinking. Jesus Christ loves you. Right now Jesus loves us as much as He possibly can! He cannot love you more, and He won't love you less, when we stumble and fall. It's a true agape love. "Heavenly father, I just pray that you'll give this world a revelation of how much you truly love them. Lord, I ask you to show them how much you love them today. I just plead the blood of the Lamb over everyone that reads this and their families. I asked for abundant blessings to come upon them in the precious name of your son Jesus Christ. Amen." God bless you today my friends."

- "Without the Holy ghost, I don't have the power to blow the fuzz off of a peanut!!!"

- "I know you have been rejected by others, you have been overlooked and passed over time after time. You have been used and abused. You lost faith in people and in love. You have a hardened heart. You have so much unforgiveness. You've been hurt so much you don't let anyone in your life, you're afraid that you'll be hurt again. But I tell you this there's only one person that will never hurt you, never deceive you, never leave you. He is the alpha and the Omega, the first and the last, the way, the truth, and the life and He's been waiting for today, just for you!!!. He's standing right beside you, with arms wide open. He has sent many people along your path, but instead of listening to what they said, you rolled your eyes and criticized them under your breath. But He forgives you. Jesus Christ loves you, and He wants a relationship with you today. He knows everything you've done and every thought you've had. And He is saying, I love you and I forgive you. Turn to him and say "Dear Jesus, please forgive me of my sins." That simple prayer will free you from the shackles and burdens of the past. "Heavenly Father, I delivered this message as you put on my heart. I pray for this individual. Let them know in their heart, Lord they can contact me as much as possible and as often as possible any time they want. I pray you'll keep your angels camped around them. I plead the blood of lamb over them. In the precious name of Jesus I pray Amen." Jesus Christ loves you so much and so do I."

- ""A merry heart does good, like medicine, But a broken spirit dries the bones." Proverbs 17:22 NKJV Right here in the Bible Laughter is the best medicine. God bless you."

- "The lack in your life is because of your lack of obedience, God puts you in that career field for a reason. Do you ever wonder why that door never shuts? Don't look at the job situation as it doesn't pay very well. The hours are bad. You gotta ask yourself, Does it pay better than sitting at home making nothing? God's not going to give you something big until he can see how you handle something small. Look at King David, he was a Shepherd boy, but those five stones and that slingshot was the start of him being a mighty king. In my own life, my obedience to hearing God's voice has allowed me to be able to see God Heal many and set many free. But my ministry didn't start out this great. My first step was to be obedient to just hear the voice of God, then I had to be obedient to pray for someone. And it just got greater and greater because of my obedience. Please don't let the devil steal what God has given you. I'm not sure who this is for, but I'm praying for you. May you have a great day. God bless."

- "Hey Billy, I really enjoy your prayers and posts. I didn't realize you were such a strong Christian. I love it! Keep up the great work, as us Christians have a lot of work to do for Him! Society is slipping away! Preach on brother." I got this message this morning, it really made my day. I post things that Jesus puts on my heart during prayer or when I am just alone with him. Jesus Christ is the greatest high I have ever been on and I want to spread his love with others. Thank you Lord for giving me the opportunity to help others and thank you for my new friend Jayson. I pray you'll open the doors of heaven and pour down blessings on him and his family in the blessed name of JESUS, I pray. Amen"

Thank Yous

This final page is dedicated to all the special men and women who had such an impact in my life, and that has helped me out in one way or another. We all have special people that have helped us in our Journeys in life. Let's take a few moments of silence and just meditate on all the great people that helped you get to where you are today. Some of those people may be with you still and some may have gone home. Just reminisce and think back of all those great people that encouraged you, lifted you up, and made you the person you are today.

A heartfelt thank you, first goes to the Great and Almighty God. I am nothing without him, my existence and being is all owed to Him. I will continue to Glorify Him and speak of His mighty name to the lost until my last breath. Without him this book would not have been written. In no specific order, each one of these people in one way or the another have led me and guided me to the good news of Jesus Christ. They've all been some kind of mainstay in my life and always keep me focused on the Almighty. They have all reminded me that I'm not perfect and I will struggle and stumble, but with a loving God, He will always pick me up, dust me off, and love on us more. He will wipe away the teardrops from our eyes. Thank you all so much for making me who I am today. May God bless you abundantly and one day we'll walk together on the streets of gold. Sincerely and with love, God Bless You.

William "Billy" C Davison III

A huge Thank You goes out to all of the following wonderful people.

The Trinity (the Father the Son and the Holy Spirit) - Irene Davison - Bill and Jane Davison - Chuck and Linda Russell - Cheryl and Gary Hughes - Debbie, Tammy, and Kelli Hughes - Terrie Kay Davison - Michael and Barbara Floyd - Tanisha, Taylor, and Dusty Davison -Donna Schmidt Hood - Megan Thomas - Marge Woods - Tom Elgi - Doug and Tricia Kuster - Mary Hayduk - John Carver - Angela Carver - Helen Diecko - And Everyone that I have crossed paths with in my journey of life with Christ, that I did not mention thank you. I thank God for all of you, thank you for helping me stand back up when I have fallen. God bless you all.

"In a moment, in the twinkling of an eye, at the last trump: for the trumpet shall sound, and the dead shall be raised incorruptible, and we shall be changed." 1 Corinthians 15:52 (KJV)

God Bless you. Jesus Christ loves you and so do I.

Sincerely,
Billy Davison

Printed in the United States
By Bookmasters